Essay Guide

Mike McClenathan

ISBN: 978-1491007648

© 2013 Mike McClenathan. All rights reserved.

No part of this book may be reproduced without prior written permission from the author to do so.

"SAT" and "SAT Reasoning Test," are registered trademarks of the College Board, which has had nothing to do with the production of, and does not endorse, this work.

For more SAT prep resources by Mike McClenathan, visit pwnthesat.com.

Table of contents

0. About everything

What I've tried to do here is to give you a clear picture of the essay's place in the SAT universe and provide some helpful advice on how to attack it. Every tutor has a slightly different approach to the essay; I don't claim that the approach herein is the only way to get a good score. I've had success with it, though, and that's reason enough to add my name to a long list of people who have put their thoughts about the SAT essay down in a book. My hope is that you'll think critically about my advice, and incorporate the tips that work for you into your SAT essay writing, and maybe even your non-SAT writing.

Rather than spilling a ton of ink and killing a bunch of trees to summarize works of literature and historical events you might like to use as evidence in your essays, I've used footnotes throughout this text to refer you to relevant further reading online. You needn't type in every URL—it's best to use examples that are meaningful *to you*—but if one catches your eye, I encourage you to seek out more information.

I've also included some URLs to pages right on the College Board's own site. The College Board's content can be dry and boring, but the College Board is the authority on its own test, and sometimes it's useful to get some information directly from the horse's mouth.

Finally, since vocabulary is **inextricably** linked to the SAT, I'll be using bold type for words I think are worth your while to learn. I strongly advise you to look these words up if you don't know them. It might not be a terrible idea to make flashcards.

About Mike

I'm an SAT tutor in New York. I've been at it for a while and I'm quite proud of my results. I started PWNtheSAT.com, where kids can get good, free test prep advice, and I've also published the *PWN the SAT Math Guide,*[1] which is about 350 pages long, contains hundreds of practice problems, and took months and months of my life that I'll never get back. It was worth it because people seem to think it's pretty good, but seriously, that was hard work!

---

[1] http://mathguide.pwnthesat.com

1. Wait…There's an essay on this test?

In my travels, I've heard a lot of misinformation about the SAT essay. So it's probably a good idea that we start our journey together by **disabusing** you of some of the more common myths, and replacing them with cold, hard, facts. Sound good?

I know. It sounds *so* good.

What this chapter covers:

- The essay's most basic attributes
- What the essay assignment looks like
- How the essay is scored
- How your essay score affects your overall writing score
- How else the essay might matter

I used to tell a joke when I would proctor a diagnostic exam for a room full of kids. "The first part of the SAT," I'd say, failing to conceal my mischievous grin, "is the es-say." Nobody ever laughed. Many groaned. And still, I couldn't resist putting it in right here in the beginning of this book. That probably says something about me. I don't know what.

Anyway, the essay is always the first section of the exam. Many people like it this way—the essay is very different from all of the other tasks you'll be required to perform on the test, so it's nice to get it out of the way. Given that you're going to have to write an essay by hand, wouldn't you rather do so while your pencil is still moderately sharp? There is a downside, however: because it comes first, the essay can set the emotional tone for the rest of the test, and it's a section in which the test writers are known to throw curve balls once in a while. You want to make sure you're ready so that you're not thrown off your game for the rest of the test.

You have twenty-five minutes to write the essay. You must write it by hand. You must write it in pencil. You get two pages, each with a bit less space to write in than you'd get if you stayed strictly inside the margins on a standard loose-leaf page. If you have a College Board *Official SAT Study Guide*[2]—you really should, by the way—turn to page 382. You must fit your essay in that. You may not color outside the lines. No smiling.

Prompts

The essay prompt consists of two components: a brief quote for context, followed by the actual essay assignment. The quote appears in a box and is sometimes attributed to a prominent thinker. Other times it's not attributed at all. It's there, ostensibly, to get your creative juices flowing if you're having a hard time getting started. Know this: *You don't have to incorporate anything from the quote into your essay.* The important thing is the assignment that comes after the quote.

In fact, because so many of your peers will be using the quote as a jumping-off point, you actually might do well to ignore it altogether and write about something other than what every other kid in the world is writing about. Doing so served a few students well when the infamous reality TV prompt[3] got everyone all riled up a few years back. The

---

[2] http://amzn.to/KpfAR8
[3] http://blog.pwnthesat.com/2011/03/on-whole-reality-tv-kerfuffle.html

quote was about reality TV, but the actual assignment asked much more broadly about entertainment. It would have been completely acceptable to write about Civil War reenactments, Colonial Williamsburg,[4] or other examples of "living history" that are obviously not real but aim to **replicate** the feel of the historical events or era they depict.

I'm going to spell out some broad categories here based on previously deployed prompts, but I want to point out before I do so that there is one universal characteristic of all essay prompts used on the SAT: *prompts ask a question to which there is no objectively provable answer.* That doesn't mean that there won't be an obvious answer *to you*; it just means that someone who disagrees with you isn't factually incorrect, just of a differing opinion. Prompts will address topics about which, as philosophers like to say, "reasonable people can disagree." It is for this reason that prompts so often tend towards classic moral questions (is it OK to lie?) and age-old social debates (can technology be bad?).

Oh, and one more **caveat**. I cannot stress this enough: *It's more important to be thoughtful and somewhat well informed than it is to be armed to the teeth with an **arsenal** of examples that cover all the **archetypal** prompts.* Writers of the SAT have proven, time and again, that they're willing to break their own mold, to the great **chagrin** of inflexible pre-planners.

I just mentioned the infamous reality TV prompt. Believe it or not, people were so **perplexed** and **incensed** by it that it made national news.[5] Students who had memorized, and were ready to **regurgitate**, carefully crafted body paragraphs for prompts about achieving goals despite **adversity** (or whatever) were **nonplussed**. Those who were nimble and

> Writing a bunch of interchangeable essay parts in advance and trying to memorize them is likely to backfire on you. Don't do it.

---

[4] http://en.wikipedia.org/wiki/Colonial_Williamsburg
[5] http://www.nytimes.com/2011/03/17/education/17sat.html

flexible—who arrived at the test center ready to think and react to the prompt—did fine.

Read over these common prompt categories, and see if you can't come up with a few pieces of evidence for each from your wealth of knowledge. If you can't come up with anything, make a note to ask your parents, friends, and teachers what they might use, or check out my evidence suggestions throughout this book. But please, treat this as an exercise in scanning your brain for ways to support arguments you might want to make. *Don't* start writing and memorizing body paragraphs. I want to help you become a good **extemporaneous** writer, not an over-prepped **automaton**.

- **Morality**
  - o Is it ever OK to lie?
  - o Should you take care of others before you take care of yourself?
  - o Should you care about people far away as much as you care about your neighbors?
- **Judging people**
  - o Is a hero someone who ___?
  - o Should we judge leaders based on ___?
- **Technology**
  - o Can technology be harmful?
  - o Have we already invented everything useful?
- **Social issues**
  - o Does everyone benefit from the success of society's highest achievers?
  - o Do people have a responsibility to care for those less fortunate than they are?
- **Creativity**
  - o Is it better to improve on old ideas or to come up with completely new ideas?

The preceding list of prompt categories is intentionally **abbreviated**, since the actual scope of what might appear on test day is so broad. If I tried to compile a complete categorization, it'd be so long as to be unwieldy, and it'd give you a false sense of security that you've thought about every possible essay prompt. You could very well get something out of left field (like the reality TV prompt) on test day, and I view it as my duty to make sure you've been warned about that possibility. So take the list seriously—it contains topics that the SAT returns to often—but remember that other topics are also fair game.

Finally, note that the College Board publishes essay prompts[6] from the most recent test date on its website. If you're looking for a realistic prompt to practice on, you can't do any better than that.

Scoring

I'm going to assume that the fact that you're reading this book indicates that you want to do well, so let's just get the ways you can score zero on your essay out of the way so that we can talk about the way essays are scored without putting an "unless" at the end of every sentence. If you don't write an essay at all, obviously that's going to earn you a zero. If you write your essay in pen, that's a goose egg, friend. If you stray from the prompt in an **egregious** way, like reproducing a pre-written essay that is clearly off-topic, that'll be a zero, too.

As long as you manage to avoid the above epic failures, the essay score you'll eventually receive will be somewhere between 2 and 12, inclusive. Here's how the sausage is made.

Your essay will be graded by two high school teachers or college faculty members who don't know each other and who probably will never meet. Neither gets to know the score the other one gave you. Each one will give you a score ranging from 1 to 6.

The scores from your two graders are added up, and that's how you get your 8, or 10, or whatever. If your score is an even number, that means your graders agreed. If it's an odd number, there was some

---

[6] http://professionals.collegeboard.com/testing/sat-reasoning/prep/essay-prompts

disagreement. If, for example, you get a 9, that means someone gave you a 5 and someone else gave you a 4. If your graders disagree about your score by more than one point—one gives you a 3 and the other gives you a 5, for example—a third grader[7] is brought in to set things right. I'm picturing someone in dark sunglasses who doesn't like small talk. This is rarely necessary.[8]

Graders take a **holistic** view of your essay, which means they're not going through it with a red pen, making marks, and tallying up the score at the end. They're getting an overall sense of the quality of your writing from a quick read, giving you a score, and moving on. That said, they are looking for a set of specific elements of good writing,[9] and those are precisely what you should be keeping in mind while you're writing your essay. In the next few chapters, we'll drill into those elements in detail.

How the essay score affects your overall writing score, and how else it's used

It's important to set the record straight about exactly what is at stake here. What do you gain by increasing your essay score? Technically, the essay is worth one third of your overall writing score, but in practice it's worth less than that. That's because the technical range of possible scores for your essay is 0 to 12, but most essays fall within a range of 6 to 10. So all the points that would come from scores 0 to 6 are basically free points for you, provided you put in the minimal effort needed to score at least a 6. Assuming your multiple-choice raw score remains constant, increasing your essay score from an 8 to a 10 will **append** about 40 extra points to your overall writing score. Increasing it from 10 to 12 will usually get you 30 more.

That doesn't seem like much, does it? That's because it's not. If you're looking for a huge overall writing score increase in a short amount of time, you'd be better off studying the grammar rules most

---

[7] Another adult to read your essay, not a child in the third grade
[8] http://professionals.collegeboard.com/testing/sat-reasoning/scores/essay
[9] http://professionals.collegeboard.com/testing/sat-reasoning/scores/essay/guide

commonly tested in the multiple-choice section. The 70 points you can gain by improving from an 8 to a 12 are, generally speaking, tougher to nail down than a 70-point increase from better multiple-choice performance. But that doesn't mean it's not worth making an effort to improve your essay writing skills. Here are a few reasons why.

Colleges you apply to might read your SAT essay

I know, right? *How come more people don't talk about this?* But it's true.[10] Some colleges will have a look-see at your SAT essays for a sense of how you write.

Isn't that what admissions essays are for? Yes, but those can be edited to death by well-meaning but misguided parents, or ghostwritten by hired guns. I know *you* would never dream of employing such tactics, but because some people do, colleges often like to get a sense of what a potential student's **extemporaneous** writing looks like.

If you're aiming for an 800 writing, you need to write a pretty decent essay

I know you're out there, 800 seekers. Scoring tables differ from test to test, but in general you can't get an 800 in the writing section with lower than a 9 on the essay. And that, of course, is with a flawless victory on the multiple-choice sections. An essay that scores higher than 9 will give you a bit of breathing room to miss an idiom question or something.

Being a good writer makes you better at life

A quick story: I had a job once where the CEO—my boss's boss's boss—would send out email blasts to the entire company. His grammar was awful. It was just **atrocious**. I would sit at my desk and read these emails and shake my head. *This is the guy who's running*

---

[10] https://nsat.collegeboard.org/diweb/login.jsp

the show? Eventually, the company went bankrupt, and we all got fired. The end.

The truth is, much of what we're going to cover in this book is good practice for the SAT essay specifically, but also good practice for writing in general. And being a good writer, in general, will make you more successful in college, in applying for jobs, and in getting hot dates. Even if you're planning to go into a career in science or engineering, you're going to be forced to write all the time, for the rest of your life. Learn to embrace it.

2. Essay Star

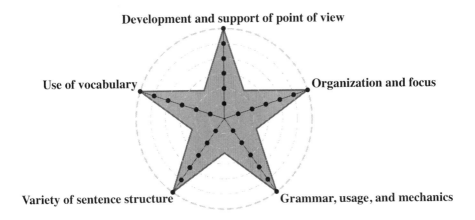

Development and support of point of view

Use of vocabulary

Organization and focus

Variety of sentence structure

Grammar, usage, and mechanics

Let's be honest here. I'm not a professional designer. I don't really have a good eye for what looks cool and what looks stupid. But I think this Essay Star is a great way to illustrate a few things about the essay.

How it works

The five axes represent the five categories upon which your essay is evaluated. The concentric rings represent scores of 1–6.

To illustrate: the sample star below shows an essay that uses 6-worthy vocabulary, but only has 4-worthy organization and focus. If you average out the category scores this essay received, you get (6+6+5+4+4)÷5 = 5. That even 5 means this essay would probably get a total score of 10 from two graders.

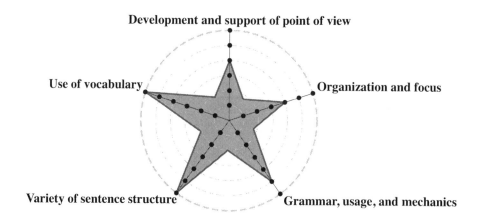

What I love about the Essay Star is that it shows how many different ways there are to reach the same final score. Students are often mystified when they receive 8s, and compare their essays to other essays that were given the same score. "This essay's grammar is so awful," they'll say. "How can it have received the same grade as mine?"

The Essay Star helps explain how. You might have grammar locked down, but if your sentences all have the same structure and you don't use any interesting vocabulary, then you're going to get the same score as a kid who tried to add some **flourish** to his essay but in so doing made a few glaring mechanical errors. If you want to score above your current level, then you need at least three of your star points to extend beyond their current ring. *What star points are holding you back?*

A corollary to the above is that this diagram also illustrates just how good an essay needs to be to get a score of 12. There are a lot of ways to get an 8, fewer ways to get a 10, and fewer still to get a 12.

To get a 12, you basically need to nail all your points. One tiny grammar error won't kill you, but much more than that and you can kiss your 12 goodbye.

A final note: The Essay Star is obviously *not* a perfect system. As we discussed earlier, graders view your essay holistically and make a judgment on their overall impression of your composition, so this star *is not* a replica of their scoring system or anything like it. Further, graders are human, so no amount of training can make them completely consistent. You might get one who values argument over all else, or you might get a grammar **stickler**.

But you can't control those things, and the Essay Star is meant to help you think about your own strengths and weaknesses, which you *can* control. As you read through this chapter, think about what your star might look like, and focus on filling it out in the way that will help your essay score the most.

At the end of the book, we'll use the star to illustrate the strengths and weaknesses of sample essays, and in so doing, identify the opportunities to improve those essays. For now, here are notes about each axis on the star, and some brief sample sentences.

Development and support of point of view

SAT essay assignments require you to take a position and support it using "reasoning and examples taken from your reading, studies, experience, or observations." In other words, you can't just say what you believe. You need to try to persuade your reader to agree with you, or at the very least convince him or her that you have good reasons for believing what you do.

You accomplish this by crafting a well-formed argument, and not overstepping the scope of the assignment. That means you establish your position, and then you support it with good evidence. Remember that, because of the murkiness of the topics essay assignments usually cover, you're not usually going to be able to craft ironclad proofs or derive universal truths. Be conscious of the strength of your premises, and make sure you draw an appropriately **qualified** conclusion.

Resist the temptation to make your argument seem stronger than it is with words like "always," "definitely," "completely," "never," etc. Far from **bolstering** the strength of your essay, these extremes have a **deleterious** effect. They make it seem as though you don't have enough faith in your argument to let it stand on its own without these crutches. They call attention to your argument's weaknesses. They challenge the reader to prove you wrong.

Instead, own up to the fact that you are limited by the time you have to write the essay and the scope of the prompt, and make a solid case for your position based on a few pieces of evidence. A **nuanced**, narrow argument will trump a failed attempt at **incontrovertible** truth every time.

Please note that I am *not* encouraging you to take both sides of an argument here. I've seen a few people do so effectively, but I don't really think there's time or space for that on the SAT essay, so I don't advise it. *You need to take a position.* I'm just saying it should be a thoughtful one.

Examples

Below you'll find two sample introductory paragraphs for an essay about the importance of honesty. Note how easily a **contrarian** could refute the first thesis, and how much more difficult it would be to do so to the second thesis. Note also that historical accuracy isn't all that important on the SAT—while the second essay might turn heads with its correct use of "**apocryphal**," the first essay would not be penalized for failing to mention that the story about the cherry tree is of **dubious veracity**.

Bad: *Lying is always wrong, and examples that prove this can easily be found in history, literature, and my own life. When George Washington was a boy and cut down a cherry tree, he told the truth about it and later became the first President of the United States. When my older brother lied to our mother about where he was going last Saturday night, and then got caught, he got grounded for a week.*

Good: *Although there are occasions in which it might be advisable to lie, those who make the truth a priority are more likely to earn the admiration of their peers. George Washington, the first President of the United States, was so admired for his honesty that the* **apocryphal** *story of the cherry tree is one of America's most well known folktales. In contrast, my older brother disappointed my mother last weekend when he failed to tell the truth about his plans.*

Organization and focus

This is a bit of a cliché, but you really should hold your reader's hand and guide him through your essay. Avoid reader whiplash at all costs—your grader should never have to pause to wonder how he got to where he is, because you should be there at every juncture, reminding him exactly where he came from and where he's going. Each sentence should flow neatly from the sentence before, and into the sentence after. Each paragraph should have a topic sentence, and stick to points relevant to that topic sentence.

You accomplish this by being **meticulous** about organizing your essay. Outline carefully before you write, jotting down the topic (and maybe the topic sentence) of every body paragraph. And then, as best you can, *stick to that outline*. If you come up with a brilliant idea for your second paragraph while you're still working on your first paragraph, it's OK to **deviate** from the plan, but if you're making up your argument as you go, your consistency and **coherence** are likely to suffer, and you'll pay with a less than stellar score.

If you want your essay to have good organization and focus, you need to tell your reader what you're going to say, say it, and once in a while remind her that you said what you told her you'd say.

Examples

Below you'll find more of the same essays whose introductory paragraphs were in the last section. Note how the first writer fails to remain laser-focused on furthering his argument and inserts details that don't really help his cause. This gives the reader the impression that, at best, the writer is a bit confused, and at worst, the writer is desperately trying to fill space. Contrast that **scattershot** prose with the output of the second writer, who diligently reminds his reader at the beginning and end of each paragraph that the reason he is writing about lying brothers and dead presidents is that they are **germane** to the topic of the value of truthfulness, and then inserts enough details to contextualize his evidence, but not so many that his point is muddled.

Assignment: Is it ever better to lie than to tell the truth?

Bad: *Lying is always wrong, and examples that prove this can easily be found in history, literature, and my own life. When George Washington was a boy and cut down a cherry tree, he told the truth about it and later became the first President of the United States. When my older brother lied to our mother about where he was going last Saturday night, and then got caught, he got grounded for a week.*

After leading the Americans to victory in the Revolutionary War, George Washington became the first President of the United States. Most people have heard the story of when he was a boy and chopped down an important cherry tree. His father was very angry about the tree's demise, and asked young George who did it. George told his father that he could not tell a lie, and his father forgave him. This story is famous because it shows how it is never OK to lie. George Washington, America's first and best president, always told the truth.

My brother got in a lot of trouble with my mom last weekend when he lied about where he was going on Saturday night. He told her he was going to be sleeping at a friend's house, but really he went to a concert 45 minutes away. My mom is a police officer and she is pretty good at catching us when we don't do what she says. She caught him because she opened his duffel bag the next morning and the clothes he was wearing smelled like smoke and there was a ticket stub in his pocket. She does not like rock music (she calls it devil music) and was really mad. She took away his phone, and he has to come right home after school all week and cannot leave the house this weekend.

Good: *Although there are occasions in which it might be advisable to lie, those who make the truth a priority are more likely to earn the admiration of their peers. George Washington, the first President of the United States, was so admired for his honesty that the* **apocryphal** *story of the cherry tree is one of America's most well known folktales. In contrast, my older brother disappointed my mother last weekend when he failed to tell the truth about his plans.*

One indicator of the value people place on honesty is the reverence Americans feel for George Washington. Legend has it that long before his heroism in the Revolutionary War or his inauguration as the first

President of the United States, the young George Washington was honored for his **adherence** to the truth. He had chopped down a cherry tree for sport, the story goes, not realizing that his actions would anger his father. When the elder Washington discovered the downed tree and demanded to know who had **perpetrated** the crime, young George stepped forward and said, "Father, I cannot tell a lie. It was I who chopped down the cherry tree." That this myth persists, even though these events almost surely did not transpire, speaks to the value our society places on honesty. Teachers and parents, in recounting this story, are making an effort to encourage children to be truthful, even when lying would be easier. Therefore, the child who learns this lesson well and lives by a code of honesty will be more likely to earn society's respect.

My brother Gerald, unfortunately, could use a refresher on the fable of George Washington and the cherry tree. He recently found himself in hot water as a result of his dishonesty. Although our mother forbade him from attending a rock concert 45 miles from our home, he decided to attend the concert anyway and simply tell our mother that he was sleeping at his friend's house that night. When my mother discovered his deception, she told him that she was more disappointed than angry (and she was pretty angry). She had trusted him **implicitly**, and he had betrayed that trust. His immediate punishment was a temporarily restricted social calendar, but my mother made it clear that the lasting impact of his actions would be that he would have to earn back her trust. As it is in the society in which we live, truthfulness is valued in my family. My mother's disappointment at Gerald's dishonesty and his appointed task of earning back her trust are further *evidence that those who are honest will be better respected.*

Use of vocabulary

A good SAT essay makes appropriate use of sophisticated vocabulary. If you've been studying **assiduously** for the SAT, you've probably already been working to **augment** your vocabulary. But if all you've been doing is studying flash cards, or memorizing definitions out of a book, you're going to have to go a little bit further. That's because, on the essay, it's not about *recognizing* words, it's about *using* them. There's a big difference.

When I was about 6 years old, a big tree fell down near my house, and my father had to cut it up with a chainsaw and carry it away in small pieces. So I learned to *recognize* a chainsaw pretty well. And boy, did I love chainsaws! I could draw a picture of one. I could imitate the noise they make (VRRRR!). To this day the smell—a mixture of fuel and sawdust—brings me right back to that summer. However, I'm able to sit here now and tell you this story because, as a child, I never tried to *use* the chainsaw myself. If I had, it would have been a bad scene.

Luckily, the stakes aren't quite as high in the transition between vocabulary recognition and vocabulary use—the only possible harm that can **befall** you when you try to use a new vocabulary word for the first time is a bruised ego if you use it incorrectly and someone calls you on it. So it would **behoove** you to get some practice with any new word before **deploying** it on test day, lest you inflict the essay equivalent of a chainsaw accident on yourself. A great way to get that practice is to *use a thesaurus when you write.*

> Don't let the SAT essay be the first time you try out a new word. Only use a word on the SAT if you've used it in conversation with an adult before, and not been corrected.

When you're writing a paper for school (or a letter to your grandma, or an acceptance speech for a major award) make it your mission to *repeat as few words as possible*. If, for example, you have occasion to use the word "angry" three times, go back and replace two of them with "**chafed**" and "**irate**." If you want to use "big" more than once, use "**voluminous**," or "**hulking**," or "**colossal**." See if you're able to create a document that doesn't repeat any words that aren't conjunctions, articles, prepositions, or pronouns. If this practice becomes second nature to you, you'll be in fantastic shape to pepper your SAT essay with appropriately sophisticated vocabulary, without making it seem like you're trying too hard. You'll also, as an added bonus, be well on your way to writing with specificity and clarity.

It's a challenge to do this well! Not every word a thesaurus will provide is exactly interchangeable in every scenario; you'll need to make sure the word you're trying to use actually fits. For example, it's cool to say a house is "big," or "**capacious**," but you probably wouldn't call a house "**burly**." It's advisable, then, to use the thesaurus and dictionary **concomitantly**. Use the thesaurus for word ideas, and the dictionary to confirm that your choice actually works in context.

To summarize, *never sacrifice flow for **flair***. Skillful use of language is showing your reader that you don't paint yourself into a corner when you write—you know how to maintain the flow in your prose by varying your vocabulary where repetition would give rise to boredom or distraction. Skillful use of language is *not* shoehorning every vocabulary word you know into a few paragraphs. That's groveling. It might work sometimes on the SAT, but it's not good writing and it'll fail you on more carefully scrutinized assignments, like college application essays. If you can learn to pepper your SAT essay with appropriately sophisticated vocabulary, without overdoing it, you'll be in great shape.

Examples

Below are a few sentences illustrating some of the pitfalls associated with vocabulary: misuse, overuse, and lack of use.

> *Even if you go on to do great things, nobody will accolade you if your past is full of lies.*

This is a chainsaw accident; "**accolade**" is a noun, not a verb. You receive accolades for a job well done. You *do not* accolade someone for a job well done. "Praise" can be used as a verb or a noun. "Accolade" is a noun only.

> The matriarch of my family has sternly asseverated
> that her children must vigorously masticate every
> morsel of sustenance.

This is someone trying *way* too hard to use big words. It's OK just to say your mom tells you to chew your food carefully.

> The house was nice, and the people who lived in it
> were nice.

This is an opportunity to use a fancy word or two in place of the bland "nice." Maybe replace the first one with "spacious" or "dignified" and the second with "**congenial**" or "gracious." Those aren't even tough vocabulary words, but not only would they make the reader take notice of the writer's use of vocabulary, but they'd also convey much more specifically how the house and people were "nice." One might also consider replacing "the people who lived in it" with "its inhabitants."

Grammar, usage, and mechanics

It's not necessary to agonize over the minutia of the English language, since you're probably already doing most of it right and since minor mechanical errors (spelling, for example) are typical of first drafts and therefore mostly forgivable on the SAT essay. Innocuous stylistic decisions (like using an em dash instead of a colon) are also not going to matter one bit. However, it should come as no surprise that it's frowned upon to make the same kind of errors that are commonly tested in the SAT's multiple-choice writing sections.

Verb agreement problems are killer. Dangling modifiers jump off the page and slap graders right in the face. Comma splices make you look silly. But the most dangerous error, the one that I see most often in students' essays, is the use of plural pronouns for singular antecedents. Remember, although many audiences will let a singular "they" slide, *on the SAT writing section, "they" must always be plural, or it's wrong.* The test writers are **dogmatic** about that rule in the multiple-choice section; you'd do best to assume that essay graders are similarly rigid.

Modern word processing programs are getting pretty good at catching your grammar errors, but when you write by hand, magic jagged underlines don't appear to alert you to grammar mistakes—you have to be alert. Train yourself to pause whenever you use the word *they*, whenever you're placing a verb after a prepositional phrase, or whenever you've written a sentence that combines more than one thought. In other words, become aware of your own usage of the same structures to which your training in the multiple-choice section has taught you to be sensitive. A few well-timed self-checks can save you from costly grammar errors that might become very messy to fix, if you even spot them at all, later on. An ounce of prevention is worth a pound of cure, as the saying goes.

Examples

The purpose of this section isn't to be **exhaustive**; comprehensive reviews of SAT grammar can be found elsewhere. In the following examples, I simply aim to remind you of rules you already know, and draw your attention to common mistakes students make in their essays.

Occasionally, I'll use gray text and <u>underlines</u> in the following pages to clarify tricky points. Get ready for action!

Verbs

You're going to be using a lot of verbs in your essay—every sentence has at least one! It's in your best interest, then, to make sure you're doing the following things correctly.

Exercise an abundance of caution when using prepositional phrases, appositive phrases, or other non-essential clauses. Be equally **chary** when employing compound subjects, or placing the subject after the verb. Note that the constructions that are likely to trip you up are the same constructions the SAT uses to test your mastery of these rules. That's not a coincidence.

Verbs | Subject/verb agreement | Prepositional phrases

A preposition is a word that establishes position (in time or space) or relationship. Common prepositions include: of, for, from, at, on, about, before, after, between, with.[11] A prepositional phrase begins with a preposition, and is usually followed by a noun. What you need to remember is that prepositional phrases often make matching subjects to verbs a bit more difficult.

In the following sentences, prepositional phrases are underlined, and subject/verb pairs are in gray.

> The display case *of trophies at the top of the stairs in my father's house* is very old.

> The fight *between the Sharks and the Jets* is going to end badly.

> The previews *before the movie* were really funny.

Verbs | Subject/verb agreement | Appositive phrases (and other non-essential clauses)

An appositive phrase is placed next to a noun or pronoun to help identify, explain, or clarify it. As is true of prepositional phrases, what you really need to worry about here is that appositive phrases often

---

[11] If you Google "prepositions," you'll find numerous long lists of prepositions.

separate subjects and verbs, thereby making it a bit more likely that rushing writers make subject/verb errors.

In the following sentences, <u>appositive phrases are underlined</u>, and subject/verb pairs are in gray.

> The display case, <u>an enclosure of glass and wood in which my father showcases his many awards</u>, is very old.

> The Sharks and the Jets, <u>fictional street gangs from the musical West Side Story</u>, fight constantly.

> Previews, <u>short clips promoting movies that will be released in the future</u>, are sometimes the best thing about going to the theater.

Did you notice in the examples above that appositive phrases can contain prepositional phrases? Is your mind blown?

Verbs | Subject/verb agreement | Subject after verb

Placing the subject after the verb once in a while is a nice way to vary your sentence structure, but be careful when doing so!

In the following sentences, observe that the conventional order of the subject/verb pairs in gray has been reversed.

> Hidden in the back of the display case are my father's high school report cards.

> Often overlooked by audiences viewing West Side Story is the fact that the musical is a modern interpretation of Shakespeare's Romeo and Juliet.

> Kicking my chair all throughout the previews was a child I very badly wanted to reprimand.

When a sentence has a compound subject, the verb depends on the conjunction used to link the subjects together. If multiple things in a list separated by "and" serve as the subject of your verb, you need a plural verb, *even if all the elements in the list are singular.* If, however, the compound subject is separated by "or" or "nor," then the verb agrees with the subject closest to it.

In the following sentences, subjects and verbs are in gray, and conjunctions are underlined.

> A *baseball, a bat,* **and** *a catcher's glove were my* favorite items in the case as a child.

> *Tony, a Jet,* **and** *Maria, the sister of a Shark, fall in love in* West Side Story.

> *Either the* cat **or** *the* dog plans *to leave us a present in the hallway.*

> *Neither the* gods **nor** Chuck Norris writes *better than I.*

> *Neither* Chuck Norris **nor** *the* gods write *better than I.*

Did you notice the appositive phrases "a Jet" and "the sister of a Shark" in the second sentence?

Verbs | Verb tense

Often, multiple tenses are appropriate for a particular sentence. Make sure, however, that if you're using multiple tenses, it's for a good reason.

The following sentences use multiple tenses correctly.

I ran the marathon last year, but this year I plan to watch it on TV with a bag of Doritos in my lap.

Bruce Springsteen would eventually become one of the most celebrated artists in all of rock music, but in 1970 he was just another kid in a band trying to get noticed.

Don't overthink your tenses. If you're not sure whether a certain tense is permissible, be safe and conventional. If you're writing about events in the past (e.g. a scientific discovery made in 1880, a great sandwich you ate yesterday), use the past tense. If you're talking about present day, use the present tense.

Pronouns

As I mentioned earlier, I see a lot of pronoun errors. So get in the habit of pausing—just for one second!—before employing a pronoun.[12]

Pronouns | Antecedent/pronoun agreement

Pronouns serve as placeholders for nouns, so they must be consistent with the nouns they replace. They must also—and this is important—actually replace a noun.

Pronouns | Antecedent/pronoun agreement | What is an antecedent?

Before we discuss agreement between antecedents and pronouns, we need to talk about what an antecedent is. Quite simply, antecedents are nouns (e.g. Dave, frying pan, football game). If the thing you're trying to replace with a pronoun isn't a noun, you probably shouldn't use a pronoun.[13] The most common pronoun people use

---

[12] There are actually a bunch of different kinds of pronouns (e.g. personal, possessive, relative, reflexive, interrogative). In the spirit of focusing on common SAT essay errors and not turning this into a grammar textbook, I'm not going to be delving too deeply into these distinctions. If you're very interested in them, Google is your friend. ☺

[13] Technically, pronouns can replace gerunds, too. Gerunds are verbs ending in -ing that serve as nouns. In the sentence, "Stopping to smell the roses is important; it

without a proper antecedent is "it." When you find yourself writing "it," make sure you can point to the noun it's replacing.

In the following sentence, the pronoun "it" is used incorrectly because it has no antecedent.

> Bad: *Yesterday, I drove my car for 5 hours, and it really hurt my back.*

Even though none of your friends would look **askance** at you if you uttered that sentence, it's not grammatically correct. The "it" clearly refers to the long ride, but since the long ride is only referred to in the verb phrase "drove my car," you can't use a pronoun. How you fix an error like this is entirely dependent on your writing style, but one possibility is below.

> Good: *My back really hurt yesterday after I drove my car for 5 hours.*

Pronouns | Antecedent/pronoun agreement | Vague pronouns

Sentences (not to mention paragraphs) often have multiple nouns. In this case, if it's not clear which noun a pronoun refers to, you're creating confusion for your readers. If there's ever any doubt as to which noun a pronoun is replacing, just use the noun (or a synonymous phrase) instead of a pronoun.

The following sentences contain vague pronouns in gray.

> Bad: *John argued with his brother Steve about the controversial call in his most recent baseball game.*

---

makes you more human," "stopping" is a gerund, the subject of the verb "is," and the antecedent of the pronoun "it." However, not all -ing words are gerunds. In the sentence "I'm stopping home to change before I go out," "stopping" is not a gerund— it's just part of the verb phrase "am stopping." If you're not already super-comfortable with this concept, you should probably ignore this footnote and just stick with the advice above: don't use a pronoun unless it's replacing a noun.

> Bad: *It was unclear to witnesses whether Shelly or Marissa caused the accident, but she blamed her quite* **vehemently**.

Again, you have a lot of **latitude** in deciding how to fix these. Below are possible rewrites.

> Good: *John argued with his brother Steve about the controversial call in Steve's most recent baseball game.*

> Good: *It was unclear to witnesses whether Shelly or Marissa caused the accident, but the former blamed the latter quite vehemently.*

Rule of thumb: if a pronoun could replace more than one noun in a sentence, or even if it's just far away from the noun you mean it to replace, it's better to be specific by using the noun again or, as I did in the second sentence, other words that make it clear what's going on in the sentence.

Pronouns | Antecedent/pronoun agreement | Singular/plural

It's pretty rare to see someone replace a plural antecedent with a singular pronoun. Replacing a singular antecedent with a plural pronoun, though, that's another story: the pronoun "they" and the possessive pronoun "their" are two of the most commonly misused words in SAT essays I've read.

Unfortunately for your SAT score, **colloquial** speech and writing is **rife** with this error: many people will use "they" to refer to a singular person if the person's sex is not clear. On the SAT, and in formal writing, this is impermissible.

In the following sentences, plural pronouns are used with singular antecedents, and vice versa. Gaze upon them and weep! (Antecedents and pronouns are in gray.)

Bad: *All chess players give his or her best effort during every match*

Bad: *Your friend changed their profile picture!*

Bad: *Every coach wants their team to win.*

Luckily, these have easy fixes.

Good: *All chess players give their best effort during every match.*

"All chess players" is plural, so it's fine to use "their!"

Good: *Your friend changed her profile picture!*

"They" actually occurs in this context all the time on social media sites because the programmers don't want to offend anyone by guessing someone's sex incorrectly if they don't know it for sure. Still, it's grammatically incorrect. If you really don't know a sex, make it up.

Good: *Every coach wants his or her team to win.*

Some people don't like this construction. "Wait," they say, "aren't we talking about all coaches? Shouldn't that pronoun be plural?"

Well, yes and no. When we use the word "every," we are indeed referring to the totality of coaches, but we use singular verbs and pronouns. Think of it like this: "every coach" means we're talking about all coaches, but only one at a time. That's why the phrase is "every coach," not "every coaches." We don't write, "every coach are strict," we write, "every coach is strict."[14] Grammatically, the adjective "every" is used to talk about multiple things using singular words. Super confusing, I know.

---

[14] I almost never see students screw this up. For some reason, using singular verbs in such cases is **intuitive**, even when using singular pronouns is not.

The general rule of thumb for "every," and adjectives like it, is that your pronoun *still* must agree with the noun it replaces, even if it's preceded by a quantifying adjective that suggests more than one of those nouns. If you put a singular noun after the adjective, you must use a singular pronoun to replace it later.

In the following sentences, pronouns and antecedents are in gray, and quantifying adjectives are underlined.

> *Each student gets 30 minutes to eat his or her lunch.*
>
> *All students like pizza days at the cafeteria more than they like oatmeal days.*
>
> *Every mother thinks she has a perfect little angel for a child.*
>
> *Several mothers meet at a restaurant downtown to brag about their children.*
>
> *Pick any flavor of ice cream and I'm sure I'll like it.*
>
> *Combine both flavors and see if they are compatible.*

Pronouns | Antecedent/pronoun agreement | Personal/non-personal

When you're using a pronoun to replace names or other nouns representing human beings, make sure you use personal pronouns.

In the sentences below, antecedents and pronouns are in gray.

> Bad: *The book was about the lives of three teenagers, all of which grew up in New Orleans.*
>
> Good: *The book was about the lives of three teenagers, all of whom grew up in New Orleans.*

Do you know the difference between "I" and "me," "he" and "him," "we" and "us," etc.? Are you always comfortable choosing which to use and which not to, even when you're working within complex structure? It's easy enough to keep subjective and objective case pronouns straight by plugging them into a simple sentence:

I chased the dog around the house.
The dog chased me around the house.

He chased the dog around the house.
The dog chased him around the house.

We chased the dog around the house.
The dog chased us around the house.

...and so on. Basically, if your pronoun is chasing the dog, it's the subject, and should be in the subjective case. If the dog is chasing your pronoun, it's the object, and should be in the objective case.

Subjective case	Objective case
I	Me
We	Us
They	Them
He	Him
She	Her
Who	Whom

Things get just a little trickier when you're trying to put a pronoun in a compound subject or object (like "Jessica and I" or "Jessica and me"). Contrary to what you might remember your first grade teacher telling you, it's *not always* "Jessica and I" that must be used!

Jessica and I chased the dog around the house.
The dog chased Jessica and me around the house.

The age-old trick here—age-old because it works—is to imagine the sentence without Jessica in there gumming up the works, and use the pronoun that would work naturally in that sentence. The one time that trick won't necessarily work is when you and Jessica are hanging out in a prepositional phrase, such as in the phrase "between Jessica and me." When you're dealing with a prepositional phrase, you *always* use the objective case. So "between Jessica and me" is always right, and "between Jessica and I" is always wrong.

> Always use "me" after "between." Never write, "between Jessica and I."

Parallelism

The beautiful thing about language is that it's so flexible. J.D. Salinger and Jane Austen both wrote in English, but if you've read both you know they exhibit two very different styles. As you write, you have great freedom to create your own style too, but in order to do so you need to remain internally consistent in the decisions you make. You get to decide if you want to use a lot of infinitives or a lot of gerunds. However, if you switch rapidly between the two, that's not style—it's **mayhem**. When we talk about parallelism, we're really talking about consistency.

Parallelism | Lists

If a sentence is listing two or more things, make sure every element in the list is structured consistently.

Parallelism | Lists | Verb conjugations

In the following sentences, multiple verbs appear in lists. Note how all the gray verbs are conjugated consistently.

> *You can kill a zombie by setting it on fire, shooting it in the head, or destroying its brain in another improvised way.*

When I travel, I prefer to take the train, to fly, or to drive, in that order.

Matt Saracen takes care of his grandmother, plays on the football team, and dates the coach's daughter.

Parallelism | Lists | Preposition use

Prepositions are cool—when used correctly they can distribute over a list. They can also be repeated for every item in the list. It's really a stylistic decision that you get to make. Once you make that decision, however, *you must stick to it*. It's like how $2(x + y + z)$ is the same as $2x + 2y + 2z$, if 2 were a preposition and x, y, and z were items in a list. That's the way I think of it, anyway. Who are you calling a weirdo?

In the first sentence below, a preposition in gray distributes over a list. In the second sentence, the preposition is repeated in each list element.

A good vocabulary will take you far in your career, your education, and your personal life.

I write to you with great sadness, but also with great hope.

Parallelism | Comparisons

Make sure the things you're comparing, if you're making a comparison, are of the same kind. In other words, only compare apples to apples and people to people, not apples to oranges and people to other people's stuff.

In the sentences at the top of the next page, the things being compared are in gray. Note how the second sentence makes the comparison much more consistent.

Bad: *Even though he is only a shoe salesman, Justin's total income is higher than his boss because Justin is also an underground street fighter on the weekends.*

Good: *Even though he is only a shoe salesman, Justin's total income is higher than that of his boss because Justin is also an underground street fighter on the weekends.*

Parallelism | Miscellaneous

Here are some other things you'll need to avoid every time before you're awarded your essay-writing black belt.

Parallelism | Miscellaneous | One vs. you

Keep 'em separated. Pro tip: it's a real pain to write a whole essay in the "one" voice. The SAT essay doesn't need to be very formal, so don't be afraid to just get personal and say "you."

In the sentences below, note how it's possible to communicate the same idea in both the "one" voice and the "you" voice. ("One" and "you" are in gray.)

Bad: *Before one goes skydiving, you should take some time to think it over.*

Good: *Before you go skydiving, you should do thorough equipment inspections.*

Good: *Before one goes skydiving, one should take out an insurance plan.*

It's also fine to just avoid the whole one vs. you mess and go plural:

Good: *Before people go skydiving, they should make sure their personal affairs are in order.*

These go together like rama lama lama ka dinga da dinga dong. If you write neither, you write nor. If you write either, you write or.

This is illustrated in the following sentences. Relevant word pairs are in gray.

> *I enjoy neither hiking nor biking.*

> *I'd be happy with either mini-golf or bowling*

Comma splices

You can't tie two independent clauses together with only a comma. You just can't. If two parts of a sentence could stand alone as complete sentences on their own (hence the term independent clauses), you cannot bind them together with a comma. Here are three reliable ways to avoid comma splices.[15]

Comma splices | Conjunctions

The conjunctions available to you to fix a comma splice are as follows: For, And, Nor, But, Or, Yet, So. An easy way to remember these is the acronym FANBOYS. Note that the list above didn't include therefore or however. Those words aren't actually conjunctions, so they don't fix comma splices.[16]

---

[15] Comma splices are often called run-on sentences, and many prep materials use the terms interchangeably. My decision to only call them comma splices is deliberate; I've found that many students have been told (incorrectly) that any really long sentence is a run-on and therefore bad. It's probably best that you don't write 10-line sentences, but well-formed sentences *can* get very long and still be grammatically correct. A comma splice is always incorrect.

[16] Therefore and however are examples of conjunctive adverbs. If you're curious what the heck that means, do some Googling. For the purposes of this book, I'm deeming it sufficient to tell you they don't work to fix comma splices. If you want to use a conjunction to fix a comma splice, use one of the FANBOYS.

The following comma splice is fixed with a FANBOYS conjunction in gray.

> Bad: *I went to the beach yesterday, Peter came with me.*

> Good: *I went to the beach yesterday, and Peter came with me.*

Comma splices | Semicolons

Unlike a comma, a semicolon *requires* an independent clause on both sides to be grammatically correct.

Note how both sides of semicolon in the fixed sentence below could stand on their own as complete sentences.

> Bad: *I went to the beach yesterday, the water was freezing.*

> Good: *I went to the beach yesterday; the water was freezing.*

Comma splices | Making a clause dependent

Both of the above (especially the semicolon) are great fixes if you catch a comma splice in your essay as you review it while time is winding down because they require little to no erasing. Making a clause dependent isn't quite as **expedient**, but it's another good way to avoid **pernicious** comma splices.

> Bad: *I went to the beach yesterday, a lifeguard punched a shark in the nose!*

> Good: *At the beach yesterday, a lifeguard punched a shark in the nose!*

Dangling modifiers

When you begin a sentence with a modifying phrase—a phrase that describes something without naming it—it must be followed directly by a comma, and then the thing being described. If you fail to make that happen, you leave the modifier "dangling." Even professional writers make this mistake from time to time, but you should try to avoid it if you possibly can—a dangling modifier can really **obfuscate** the intended meaning of a sentence.

In the sentences below, modifying phrases and the things they modify are in gray.

> <u>Bad:</u> *Because he had bet on the race, the horse disappointed Mr. Johnson a great deal.*

> <u>Good:</u> *Because he had bet on the race, Mr. Johnson was greatly disappointed in the horse's performance.*

> <u>Bad:</u> *Excited for the concert, the auditorium shook with the noise from the crowd.*

> <u>Good:</u> *Excited for the concert, the crowd made so much noise that the auditorium shook.*

> <u>Bad:</u> *Fleeing the zombies, a safe-looking building appeared to the survivors.*

> <u>Good:</u> *Fleeing the zombies, the survivors spotted a safe-looking building in the distance.*

Note how the sentences in which the modifier is left dangling seem to imply strange things. A horse can't bet on a race, an auditorium can't get excited, and a building can't flee.

Variety of sentence structure

I was just **advocating heterogeneous** word use in the vocabulary section; varied sentence structure is another way sophisticated writing keeps readers interested and engaged. If every sentence is the same length, and has the same structure, readers nod off. They get lulled into a dream-like state, which makes them less likely to retain what they've read—an undesirable outcome for any writer and doubly so for SAT essay writers, who only get a couple minutes to make an impression on their readers.

To avoid putting your readers to sleep, keep an eye on the length of your sentences. If they've all been short lately, throw a long one in. If they've all been super long, make one short. Start a sentence with a modifier, or use an **appositive** phrase to keep your reader engaged.

> If you're getting bored writing your essay, you can bet your readers will be bored reading it. Mix things up!

Examples

Below you'll find an example of a paragraph that's super boring because of homogenous sentence structure, followed by a rewrite that will make its reader less likely to have to slap herself in the face to stay awake.

> Bad: *Manchester Orchestra is one of my favorite bands. Their last record came out in 2011. It's a really excellent record. It's called Simple Math. It's my favorite record the band has put out yet. My favorite song on Simple Math is called "Mighty." That's a good name for the song because it really rocks hard!*

Note how choppy that paragraph is. Each sentence has a pretty similar subject/verb structure, and each sentence is short. Let's fix it:

<u>Good:</u> *Manchester Orchestra is one of my favorite bands. 2011's Simple Math, the band's most recent record, is its best yet. The album highlight is "Mighty," which is aptly named given its driving, muscular guitar riffs. It rocks!*

That's better, right? The first sentence didn't change at all, but the second sentence contains a nice appositive phrase ("the band's most recent record"). The sentences vary in length: medium, long, long, short.

Your writing might flow like this naturally, but if you're ever accused of being choppy, take heed. It's very difficult to achieve a high essay score if your sentence structure is **plodding** and **monotonous**.

3. Structure

I'm going to break it down for you like this. First, I'm going to spend some time digging into the body section of the essay. Then, I'm going to talk about the introduction and conclusion. I know that's a bit **unorthodox**. Stay with me.

Body

I'm choosing to talk about the body before I talk about the introduction and conclusion because, quite simply, the body of your essay is more important than your introduction or conclusion. It constitutes most of your output, and therefore will win (or lose) you the most points. This is where you make your argument. The introduction and conclusion are just formalities that summarize it. And although you'll obviously have to write your introduction before you write your body, you really should think about what your body will look like before you write your introduction. More on this later.

In this section, you're going to notice me using the word "evidence" a lot, where most in the prep world would be talking about "examples." This is intentional. I want you to be thinking, as you decide how you'll support your argument, about how you'd make your case in a court of law. Examples can be flimsy in a number of ways—they can be hypothetical, for instance. Evidence, on the other hand, is firm. It supports arguments. It wins cases. You want to make the strongest argument you can, to impress upon your reader that you're a force to be reckoned with. And to do that, you'll want to rely on a strong body of evidence.

Now, let's talk about actually writing a body paragraph.

Mini-thesis

The first sentence of any body paragraph should be what I call a *mini-thesis*. This sentence should refer back to your main thesis, and put it in the context of the evidence you plan to cite in the paragraph. This shows your reader that you're focused on the question, which helps you in the organization and focus department.

There's no need to get fancy here. The point is simply to point out to your reader, before you dive into the details, that the evidence you're about to discuss is important, and not just something you were planning to write about no matter what prompt you got. It's also an opportunity for you to provide a few transitional words, so your reader doesn't get whiplash when you change gears between paragraphs. Say you're arguing that innovation happens incrementally, not all at once. You want to cite as evidence that the US Constitution[17] is an **amalgam** of various political philosophies and has evolved over time, and that the social networking **behemoth** Facebook was not invented out of the blue, but was rather inspired by social networking sites that came before it like Friendster and MySpace. These topics have gradual evolution in common, but not much else, so you should use a few words between them to acknowledge their differences and assert their similarities.

---

[17] http://en.wikipedia.org/wiki/United_States_Constitution

Assignment: Does human progress happen in fits and starts, or does innovation occur gradually over time?

> Thesis: *While it is possible to find examples of ideas that seemingly came from nowhere and changed the course of history, most new ideas evolve over time.*
>
> Mini-thesis at the beginning of body paragraph 1: *One prominent example of the evolution of ideas is the Constitution of the United States.*
>
> Mini-thesis at the beginning of body paragraph 2: *The evolution of ideas happens at a much more accelerated pace in the world of social networking.*

Your transition doesn't need to be grand or overstated. In the example above, it's just a simple acknowledgement that you're moving from the relatively slow evolution of political thought to the **frenetic** pace of technological innovation. That's plenty.

The rest of your body paragraph

Once you've established yourself with a mini-thesis, it's time to support it. Don't just repeat the claim you made in the first sentence— use relevant details to convince your reader that your claim has merit.

Be as specific as possible with the facts you cite, but don't turn this into a torrent of information. This isn't the place to just list every fact you know. Your mission is to give your reader, in a few sentences, a reason to believe that the book, historical event, personal experience, or whatever that you're writing about is relevant to your thesis. Every detail you give must **bolster** your argument.

> Be super specific, but make sure the details you're including are strengthening your argument. This is a persuasive essay, not a book report.

One prominent example of the evolution of ideas is the Constitution of the United States. Delegates to the Constitutional Convention were inspired by a vast **array** of existing philosophies. For example, the Constitution's due process clause was inspired by the Magna Carta, and its protection of the basic rights of life, liberty, and property was inspired by British philosopher John Locke's conception of the social contract. The American system of checks and balances is commonly credited to French thinker Montesquieu. The Constitution was also inspired by the guiding principles of the Iroquois Confederacy. The founding fathers **explicitly** acknowledged that ideas evolve over time by ensuring that the Constitution would be a living document that could be refined via amendment. For this reason, the Constitution that governs us today is an **amended** version of the one that was ratified in 1787, and the Constitution that governs the United States 100 years from now will be further changed as our democracy continues to evolve.

The evolution of ideas happens at a much more accelerated pace in the world of social networking. Facebook founder Mark Zuckerberg's conception of the now-**ubiquitous** service was informed by social networking services that already existed. My father argues that the profile system of AOL Instant Messenger was the original social networking site. Internet entrepreneurs recognized how much people loved to customize their AOL profiles, and created services that would allow users even more flexibility to express their personalities. These included a number of social networking sites that predated Facebook, like Friendster and MySpace—both dominant in their times *and now **consigned** to the dustbin. Facebook was able to achieve market **hegemony** over both services by emulating and improving upon their best features. Now that it dominates the social networking space, Facebook is forced to defend itself against **upstart** services like Google Plus, which seek to beat Facebook by improving on Facebook's best features, much the same way Facebook outdid its predecessors years ago. Innovation in social networking is characterized not by revolutionary technological sea changes, but rather by **incremental** improvement of existing ideas.*

Do you see all the specific details in there? In the Constitution paragraph, four specific influences were named, along with the specific year of the Constitution's ratification. In the social networking paragraph, five services were named. And note that all those details directly support the argument! The fact that four influences were named really supports the argument that the Constitution represents evolving ideas. The date of the Constitution's ratification emphasizes how long the document has been evolving since it was first signed.

If you're wondering, at this point, how you'll ever be able to squeeze that level of detail into an essay in twenty-five minutes, I feel you. It's not easy. But it becomes much more doable when you know your evidence inside and out.

The best evidence is the evidence you know well

I'm going to include a list of some commonly used references a little later on, just because it feels like a book about the SAT essay needs to include something like that, but in a way, I hope you ignore it. It's much better to write about what you know than to trot out the same tired old evidence that everyone else uses.

My friend Craig Gonzales, who does SAT tutoring in Bangkok, helps his students achieve great scores not by telling them to write about

George Washington or The Great Gatsby, but by encouraging them to write about events and issues that they, as Thai students, have a unique perspective on.

I cannot overstate how much I like this approach. You're not going to have a unique perspective on every single question that could get thrown your way, but if you think about the common prompt themes now, and think about how events near to you might be used to inform your position on those themes, you'll be setting yourself up to write from the heart about something you know well and care about. Passionate, well-informed writing trumps regurgitated plot synopses of the great books any day.

Perhaps an illustration is called for. I live in New York City. At the time of this writing, many in this area are still dealing with the effects of "Superstorm" Sandy. Some peoples' homes have been completely **obliterated**. The storm and the events that have unfolded around it are all that you hear people talking about when you pass them on the street. Here are a few things I'd be very comfortable writing about in an SAT essay.

- The New York City Marathon was scheduled to occur only a few days after the storm crippled the city. The Marathon begins in Staten Island, which bore much of the brunt of the storm and was still reeling. An emotional debate took place between those who wanted the Marathon to go on as planned and those who wanted it canceled. Those in favor of the Marathon argued that it was important for New Yorkers to return to normalcy, and pointed to the amount of revenue it generates for the city, and the fact that athletes from all over the world had spent months training, planning, and making travel arrangements for the race. Those opposed pointed to the devastation on Staten Island, claiming that not only was it in poor taste for so many out-of-towners to descend on the city for recreation at such a time, but also that the race would **divert** important public services—like police and ambulance services—from the ongoing recovery efforts to the marathon.

In the end, the Marathon was canceled. This could be a great piece of evidence to cite in an essay about whether people who think, "The show must go on," are always right.

- Sandy was a devastating tragedy, but might also present an opportunity in that it has pushed the issue of climate change into the national policy conversation. NYC Mayor Michael Bloomberg and NY Governor Andrew Cuomo both made unequivocal statements about the necessity of adapting to a changing climate in the wake of the storm. After 3 presidential debates during the 2012 campaign failed to touch on climate change at all, President Barack Obama referred to the dangers of a changing climate in his victory speech on Election Night soon after. This could be a great piece of evidence to cite in a tragedy/opportunity essay.

- New Jersey Governor Chris Christie, a Republican, publicly praised President Barack Obama, a Democrat, for his attention to New Jersey in the aftermath of the storm, mere days before a bitterly contested presidential election. This was a very unpopular move among many in Christie's party, but the Governor felt that the gravity of New Jersey's situation demanded a **reprieve** from **partisan rancor**. This could be a great piece of evidence to cite in any essay having to do with compromise, or doing what's right over doing what's popular.

These are just a few pieces of evidence from one (albeit a big one) recent event in my city that I could cite in support of a number of different arguments. What's happened lately where you live? I bet lots of things. I bet you could write about some of them.

Here are a few other things I'm passionate about that I could write about at the drop of a hat, if they fit with the prompt:

- **Bruce Springsteen:** I've actually written about Bruce Springsteen in an SAT essay before. He's one of America's great songwriters, with a catalog that spans decades and captures many elements of American culture. I'm not going to say I could work him into *any* SAT prompt, but then again I am totally saying that.

- **R.A. Dickey:** Dickey overcame childhood abuse and numerous setbacks in his professional baseball career before his historic 2012 season with the New York Mets. He was 37 years old when he had an almost miraculous season, for which he would become the first knuckleballer to win the Cy Young Award (an award given to the league's best pitcher). His is a great story of hardship, failure, **perseverance**, and triumphant redemption.
- *Argo*: I saw this awesome movie while I was working on this book, and then it went on to win a bunch of awards. It's based on a true story about a daring escape. You've probably seen it, and if you haven't you should. Either way, I'm not going to summarize the plot here. It'd work nicely in a morality essay. When is it OK to lie? When you're trying to rescue people who are in grave danger.
- **Mitch Hedberg:** My friends and I listened to Mitch Hedberg's comedy CDs *constantly* in college. Sadly, he overdosed in a hotel room in 2005, and is no longer with us. His is a story of success, excess, and not getting help that's badly needed. His story would provide a nice contrast to someone who did ask for help and thrived as a result.

I don't imagine you're as passionate about the above as I am. If you are, we should start a fan club! But if you're not, you should make a similar list for yourself. Just some cool stuff you're really into, and what kinds of essays the stuff might work in. Might come in handy.

Commonly used evidence

I don't intend to reinvent the wheel here by telling you all about these people, books, and events. All of the following citations from literature and history have been summarized hundreds of times, and they all have Wikipedia entries that provide sufficient **synopses**. This list is not meant to teach you new things; my intention is just to jog your memory about things you've already learned. And as I just finished saying, I think it's better that you write with passion about what you know than write about any of these, all of which your graders will have been exposed to hundreds, if not thousands of times.

Literature

I know I was a bit flippant about the great books just a few paragraphs ago, but the fact is that they're called great for a reason. Hopefully you've read a few of them, and hopefully some of them have resonated with you to such an extent that you can write about them passionately and convincingly.

But even if none of the classics have blown you away, they're so thematically rich that if you've read them and discussed them in class, you should know enough to use them as evidence in a two-page essay. The following is a short list of books I've seen a multitude of students write about **adroitly**. You're likely to have read at least a few of these as part of your studies; it'd be a good use of your time to remind yourself of the major plot points and character names of those you have read before SAT day so that they're on your mind if they would help support your argument.

If you've read *The Hunger Games* and, like, totally loved it, you might be able to use it if you get the *perfect* prompt (like one about how power corrupts, or whether it's good to stand up for what you believe in, or why training children to murder each other is bad). Don't write about *Twilight*.

As a final note, I'd advise you strongly against writing about books if you have no idea what happened in them. Remember, your graders are English teachers of some kind, so they have probably read most of the books that you've been assigned in high school. You don't have to get

> If you haven't actually read a book, don't use it as evidence.

every detail right, but if you argue that *Macbeth* ended well for the title character, it's going to be very difficult for your grader to give you a high score. Spoiler alert: He dies in the end. Violently.

Classic literature that's good for the SAT essay includes (in no particular order):

- **Great books:** *The Scarlet Letter, Moby Dick, Jane Eyre, The Great Gatsby, The Grapes of Wrath, Lord of the Flies, The Crucible, Walden, The Adventures of Huckleberry Finn, To Kill a Mockingbird, Animal Farm*
- **Shakespeare:** *Macbeth, Hamlet, Romeo and Juliet*
- **Contemporary classics:** *The Things They Carried, One Flew Over the Cuckoo's Nest, The Kite Runner, The Namesake*
- **Teen angst classics:** *The Catcher in the Rye, A Separate Peace*
- **Dystopian futures:** *1984, Brave New World, Fahrenheit 451*

History and current events

If you choose to go the history route, try to write about events that you've studied in school and therefore have some experience writing about and placing in historical context. Use the lists below to re-familiarize yourself with the details of some commonly cited pieces of evidence if it's been a while since you studied them.

- **The American Revolution:** Thomas Jefferson, Benjamin Franklin, George Washington, Nathan Hale, Benedict Arnold, The Boston Massacre, The Battle of Trenton (Christmas 1776)
- **The American Civil War:** Abraham Lincoln, The Emancipation Proclamation, The Gettysburg Address, Ulysses S. Grant
- **The American Civil Rights Movement:** Martin Luther King, Jr., Rosa Parks, Brown v. Board of Education, Malcolm X…
- **World War II:** Don't use Hitler. Just don't.
- **Indian Independence Movement:** Mahatma Gandhi

Don't limit yourself to these events! They're just an **infinitesimal** sampling of the richness of human history. If at all possible, try to write about historical events that have personal significance for you.

If you decide to cite current events, remember that your graders are human, and have opinions. Even though they're supposed to suppress their biases and be impartial when they read your essay, it's probably best that you steer clear of recent events that might be controversial. If you write about Barack Obama, who at the time of this writing has just won reelection with 51% of the popular vote, you've got a roughly 49% chance that your reader recently voted against him. The 2012 campaign season was incredibly **caustic**, and feelings about the election might be raw for a long time.

I'm not going to say you *can't* write about current politics or other **contentious** issues—my own Hurricane Sandy examples earlier are pretty political—but do so only if you think you can maintain some **semblance** of **impartiality**. If your essay devolves into **ideological** cheerleading, you'll be on thin ice. For example, if I were to actually use the example I just mentioned about Governor Christie and President Obama, I would be careful not to reveal in my essay which political party I support. Instead, I would focus narrowly on the reality that Christie's **overtures** to Obama in those days after Sandy were unpopular with his own party at the national level, and argue that Christie nevertheless did the right thing for his state when he gave the President a warm welcome.

Other

Of course, there are plenty of great pieces of evidence that come from places other than history or literature. There are great films and plays; sports figures, musicians, and other celebrities; and yes, your own personal experience. Be creative! I've read convincing essays about all of the following:

- Lance Armstrong's historic victories at the Tour de France (or his **subsequent** fall from grace as he became buried under doping **allegations**)
- Pat Tillman, who left a promising career in the NFL to become an Army Ranger, and was killed by friendly fire in Afghanistan
- *Saving Private Ryan*

- Angelina Jolie's **philanthropy**
- Weightlifting, sports training, piano practice, etc.
- A parent or other relative who lost a job, didn't despair, and then found a better job

Hopefully the previous few pages have reminded you of a few potential pieces of evidence you know well, or inspired you to come up with your own list. If that list of yours is still a bit **anemic**, here are a few further questions to ask yourself to help you fill it out:

- Who are my heroes?
- What have I read about in the news (or seen on YouTube) recently that's inspired me?
- What specific difficulties challenge my family, and how do we overcome them?
- Has there been a time when a community I belong to has rallied around a cause?

Remember, you're at your best when you write with passion and authority, but to do that, you need to support your argument with **copious** evidence.

Introduction and conclusion

It might drive you crazy that these two different sections are lumped under one heading. And of course they're different. But they're also the same: in the **proverbial** essay sandwich, both introduction and conclusion are bread. If you'll **indulge** me in continuing with the sandwich metaphor for a bit longer, an open-faced sandwich is OK! You don't always need that last piece of bread to top it off. While you might always plan to write a conclusion, you must remember that it's the least important component of your essay. If you find yourself running out of time and you're considering **truncating** a body paragraph to write a conclusion, *don't*. A **marginally** more developed body paragraph showcases a little bit more critical thinking. A

> Remember, you're scored on the quality of your argument, not whether you wrote a conclusion.

conclusion just says the same thing you already said in your introduction; it adds nothing new to your essay. Remember, you're graded on the quality of your argument, not on whether you wrote a conclusion.

Introduction

Many students try to gussy up their introductions with broad, sweeping generalizations about life, or meditations on the definition of words, or some other clever "hook." I've realized in my years of tutoring that this habit dies hard—students have labored for years under the assumption that they need to open every essay with a statement of undeniable **profundity**, lest their audience drift elsewhere. Let's just lay it on the table: SAT essay graders are going to give your essay the same 90–180 seconds whether you hook them or not, so you shouldn't waste precious time (or space) trying to do so. You're being graded on whether you craft an effective argument, not whether you open your essay with **axiomatic** pizazz. Get. To. The. Point.

Thesis

Your first sentence should state your position clearly. *Take a defensible position, and state it in clear, bold terms.* When I say your thesis should be defensible, I basically mean that you shouldn't try to do too much—if you try to arrive at some deep philosophical truth in your essay, you'll leave yourself open to obvious **rebuttal**. Your grader will focus more on why you're obviously wrong than she will on how nicely you incorporated some nice vocabulary into your essay, and your score will suffer for it. It might be best to illustrate this by example.

Assignment: Is it important to remain true to one's convictions?

> Trying to do too much: *Firmly held positions are unreasonable.*

Here's what your grader is thinking when you make a statement like that: "Martin Luther King, Jr.'s firmly held positions were pretty reasonable. So were Galileo's. *So are mine.*" All you wanted to do is argue in favor of flexible thinking, but now you've trapped yourself into arguing that there are no positions that one can reasonably hold firmly. That's a difficult philosophical argument to make.

Assignment: Is it important to remain true to one's convictions?

> Defensible position: *It is more important to be open-minded than It is to be true to one's convictions.*

Note how I'm not saying that it's not important to be true to your convictions. I'm only saying that it's more important to be open-minded. This makes it much harder for a reader to immediately dismiss my position out of hand.

Note also that the position above is stated in clear, bold terms. Don't muddle your thesis with unnecessary qualifications. Don't preface it with a direct answer to the prompt—you're asked a question but you do not need to say yes or no. Resist the urge to write "I think" or "my opinion is."

Now, let's add some nuance.

The rest of your intro

Spend the rest of your introduction (2–4 more sentences) clarifying your thesis, if need be, and giving your reader a preview of the rest of your essay by mentioning the evidence you plan to analyze. Here's the full intro paragraph I started above:

Assignment: Is it important to remain true to one's convictions?

> *It is more important to be open-minded than it is to be true to one's convictions. While society tends to lionize those who remain true to their convictions, it does so*

*only for people whose convictions it judges to be right. People who hold their positions firmly run the risk of being wrong, and therefore remembered as fools or villains, rather than heroes. Many consider longtime US Senator Strom Thurmond a **malevolent** figure in American history because of his **dogmatic** opposition to civil rights. On the other hand, Amazon.com CEO Jeff Bezos believes that his success can be attributed in part to his flexibility and willingness to change his mind.*

Here's the nuance: I'm setting my essay up to support my thesis from two angles. First, I'll use a figure from history whose reputation suffered for his hardheadedness—the late US Senator Strom Thurmond,[18] who famously cemented his place on the wrong side of history when he **filibustered** the Civil Rights Act of 1957. Then I'll contrast Thurmond with a generally respected, wildly successful person who believes in being flexible—Amazon.com CEO Jeff Bezos.[19] Bezos has played an important role in revolutionizing 21st century commerce, and he attributes his success in part to his ability to see issues from multiple angles and change his mind.

This, by the way, is why you should outline a bit before you write anything. *Your evidence should inform your thesis.* When you've already decided what evidence you want to cite, you can craft a nuanced, defensible position that your evidence supports perfectly!

> When you outline first, you enable yourself to craft a thesis statement your evidence can easily support.

Note how the last two sentences not only mention the people I'm going to use as evidence by name, but also focus on the particular aspects of these two men that I think support my thesis. Remember: It's pretty much impossible to be too specific in an SAT essay.

---

[18] http://en.wikipedia.org/wiki/Strom_Thurmond
[19] http://37signals.com/svn/posts/3289-some-advice-from-jeff-bezos

Conclusion

Honestly, as long as you've done a good job on all the parts leading up to this one, there's very little left you need to accomplish here. Your mission, in your conclusion, is very simply to remind your reader of how incredibly convincing you have been. The biggest danger here is that you overdo it by expanding your scope, or by claiming you've accomplished something you haven't. To avoid overdoing it, simply take one to three sentences to restate your thesis in slightly different words.

Assignment: Is it important to remain true to one's convictions?

> The **tarnished** legacy of the close-minded Senator Thurmond highlights the danger of holding convictions too strongly. By contrast, the great success of Jeff Bezos indicates the value of being open to changing one's mind. The stories of both men suggest that it is more important to be open-minded than it is to hold one's convictions firmly.

Again, resist the urge to oversell in your conclusion. This means you shouldn't claim that you've *proven* anything! You haven't. All you've done is made what you hope is a pretty convincing argument in support of the thesis you carefully crafted in your introduction.

> Whenever you're tempted to write *prove*, use words like *suggest*, *support*, or *indicate* instead.

As I noted above, your conclusion is the least important part of your essay. Therefore, if you're short on time or space, it's the first thing you should be willing to **jettison**. Don't cut your body short to get to a conclusion. If you haven't said everything you want to say in your body yet, you're better off running out of time (or space) without a conclusion but with a slightly more refined argument due to your additional **explication** of evidence.

Skeleton

To following essay skeleton summarizes the chapter you've just read (carefully, I'm sure). It might be a good idea to dog-ear this page for quick review.

1. *Introduction paragraph* (2–5 sentences)
    i. Sentence 1 is your thesis. Waste no time getting to it!
    ii. If you like, you can use another sentence or two to elaborate a bit on your thesis and make it stronger. If you're going to argue that hard work is necessary for success, for example, then maybe you make your second sentence something about failure stemming from lack of hard work. In doing so, you strengthen your thesis a bit by approaching it from multiple angles.
    iii. In the last sentence or two, mention the evidence you plan to cite so your reader knows what's coming.
2. *Evidence 1 paragraph: Your best piece of evidence*
    i. Sentence 1 is a mini-thesis. Basically, it introduces your first piece of evidence again and relates it directly to your main thesis.
    ii. The rest of your sentences are a mix of relevant details (if your evidence is from a piece of literature, for example, then you need to mention relevant plot points) and gentle reminders to your reader that these details support your thesis. See if you can reference your thesis in some way at least twice in this paragraph. The outline you jot down before you start writing should have at least three bullet points for relevant details you want to include. (We'll talk more about outlining in the next chapter.)
3. *Evidence 2 paragraph: Your second best piece of evidence*
    i. Sentence 1 is, again, a mini-thesis. This one should, however, also contain some kind of transition. Example transition from literary evidence to a personal experience, on the topic of careful planning for important events: "Like the Joad family in Steinbeck's The Grapes of Wrath, I was once forced to leave

my home because of a natural disaster, so I know firsthand the value of careful planning."

    ii. The rest of this paragraph should again be a combination of relevant details and pointers back to the main thesis. If this paragraph is a little shorter than the last one, that's fine, but make sure you still cram in as much specificity as possible.

4. *Conclusion paragraph* (1–3 sentences, if you include one at all)

    i. Don't introduce any new information here. Just wrap your essay up with a few sentences by reminding the reader once more what your thesis is, and that your carefully chosen supporting evidence is strong support for that thesis.

4. Actually writing the essay

It's important to state again here that there's no one single way to write a good essay; there are many paths to a good score. However, I've found that the following procedure and format produce reliably good results. In this chapter, I'm going to describe the process you should follow to write your essay, from start to finish.

Plan

Before you write a single word on your essay paper, you should spend 2–4 minutes mapping out your argument. The process might seem a bit burdensome at first, but 1) it'll get easier with practice, and 2) it's worth practicing because it'll make you a more convincing and more consistent writer.

Step 0: Read the prompt

Duh. You obviously have to do this. Begin by reading the actual question, not the excerpt above it. If your mind starts racing immediately with relevant current events or books you might want to reference, that's great! You might not even need to read the excerpt. If, after reading the prompt itself, you feel like you could use a bit of inspiration, read the excerpt.

Step 1: Brainstorm evidence

This is important, and not intuitive at first. You need to consider the evidence you'll cite *before* you can wisely choose your position. That's because this is not an essay about your personal feelings and beliefs. This is an essay in which you are making an argument. And if you want to present a convincing argument, you need good evidence.

Make a rudimentary t-table on the assignment page with two columns—one labeled "yes," where you'll jot down some evidence that supports an affirmative response to the prompt, and one labeled "no," where you'll put evidence that contradicts the "yes" stuff.

You'll eventually use this table to pick your position, but for now really try to fill in both sides as best you can. This is how you'll figure out which side you'll be most successful arguing. But note that there's also value in having thought of a few things to put in the column you don't end up choosing for your position: you've spent a bit of time thinking how someone who disagrees with you might attack your argument, which will help you write a more convincing essay.

> Even if you don't address them directly in your essay, it's good to have considered likely arguments against your position.

Say you were given the following prompt:

Physically, morally, and emotionally we are woven into the web of life with old-growth redwoods and rainforests and dying lakes and polluted rivers. We need them, not simply as a matter of intelligent resource management, but for the good of our souls. The same toxins that kill them run in our blood, the ugliness of their suffering afflicts our eye, for all we know images of their dire fate haunt our dreams. And surely children who grow into life without knowing wild nature will be less than fully human.

Adapted from Theodore Roszak, "Sanity, the psyche, and the spotted owl"

Assignment: Does one's emotional wellbeing partially depend on one's environment? Plan and write an essay in which you develop your point of view on this issue. Support your position with reasoning and examples taken from your reading, studies, experience, or observations.

Your "yes" column is going to be evidence that suggests that one's emotional wellbeing *does* depend on one's environment, and your "no" column is going to be evidence that suggests the opposite. You might come up with something like this:

Yes	No
(emotional health depends on environment)	(emotional health is independent of environment)
Seasonal Affective Disorder - form of depression - mostly occurs in winter - lots of people have it Solitary confinement - Seen as a very harsh punishment for prisoners Animals in captivity - Orcas' dorsal fins fold over in captivity Thoreau's *Walden*	My brother - stays inside all day playing Xbox - seems happy enough

Step 2: Choose your position

If the above is what you've come up with, then your decision is made for you—known psychological disorders and dreaded prison punishments are stronger evidence than your brother's video game habits. You should probably decide to argue that one's emotional wellbeing depends on one's environment—*whether that's actually consistent with your beliefs or not.*

Step 3: Write your thesis

I won't rehash everything I wrote about thesis writing here. It was just last chapter! You must remember.

You're not writing your thesis on the actual essay paper yet. This is just going to become the first line in the outline you'll construct in the next step, and it's a chance for you to see your thesis written out and give it a critical look before committing it to your essay sheet.

Don't forget to be thoughtful, and take a nuanced, defensible position.

Step 4: Outline

You don't need to go crazy here, but before you start writing your essay, you should set a few guideposts for yourself. This will keep you on point, and spare you from that awkward feeling you get when you think a paragraph needs more, but you can't think of anything else to say. Here's what an outline should look like, in general:

- **Thesis**
- **Evidence 1**
  - o **Detail 1**
  - o **Detail 2**
  - o **Detail 3 (If possible)**
- **Evidence 2**
  - o **Detail 1**
  - o **Detail 2**
  - o **Detail 3 (If possible)**

That's it. Nothing earthshattering there. Note that there aren't bullets for the introduction or conclusion. Those are supposed to be short and not include much detail, and it's not like you're not going to forget to write them (except if you run out of time and don't do a conclusion, *which is no big deal*), so they don't need to be included in an outline.

Here's what an outline might look like given the t-table above.

- **Thesis:** Although many factors surely contribute, one's environment can play an important role in determining one's emotional health.
- **Evidence 1:** Thoreau's *Walden*
  - o **Detail 1:** Brief description
  - o **Detail 2:** Contrast with Industrial Revolution
  - o **Detail 3:** Thoreau's contentedness and how people react to *Walden*
- **Evidence 2:** Seasonal affective disorder
  - o **Detail 1:** Define SAD
  - o **Detail 2:** Advertisement on TV

There are a few points I want to make here. First, note how the writer's thinking has focused slightly since brainstorming. He's decided that the last thing he thought of in his brainstorm, Thoreau's *Walden*, is his strongest, and therefore leading, piece of evidence. He's also deciding to cut out the bit about animals in captivity and solitary confinement of human prisoners, and write about seasonal affective disorder, which he thinks he can use to make a strong point despite not being an expert on the subject.

Also, note how this essay will argue the thesis from two angles: it'll show the pleasures of a pleasant environment with the Thoreau bit, and then talk about the negative effects of an unpleasant environment. That's good hustle.

Further, note that this is a tough prompt; it seems to have thrown our writer for a bit of a loop. He might have written about *Walden* before even though he didn't think of it immediately, but he probably hasn't ever written an essay about a psychological disorder he knows very little about. This is OK. It might have taken him a minute more than usual to brainstorm and outline, but he'll be able to put together a totally workable essay with this material. At any rate, he'll do much better this way than he would if he tried to philosophize for two pages.

Lastly, note how easy the essay will be to write from this outline. Outlining *does* take time—you should plan your essay for three to four minutes before you start writing. But if you're outlining well, you're making the actual essay writing easier for yourself.

Write

Once you've created a solid outline, then all that's left to do is actually write the essay. Since you've already decided where it's going to go and what it's going to say, though, the actual writing should come easily—it should feel like connecting the dots. Here's the final result our writer came up with after the outlining he did above:

Although many factors surely contribute, one's environment can play an important role in determining one's emotional health. Evidence suggests not only that a pleasant environment can benefit a person's mental health, but also that a negative environment can have a deleterious effect on one's emotional wellbeing.

Henry David Thoreau's Walden, *a widely read account of the simple life, illustrates man's intimate connection with his environment. The book is Thoreau's account of the time he spent at Walden Pond, where he lived in a* **spartan** *cabin, contemplated his surroundings, and meticulously recorded his experience. The resulting volume has achieved lasting prominence not only because of Thoreau's eloquence, but also because it was written during a time when much of the world around* **bucolic** *Walden Pond was becoming much less* **serene***. Thoreau's retreat to nature was not necessarily a response to the* **nascent** *Industrial Revolution and the soot,* **clamor***, and* **consumerism** *that came with it. But* Walden*'s publication came at a time when many were questioning whether the Industrial Revolution was really as great as advertised. The book's* **robust** *sales in the 19th century, and its continued* **prominence** *in high school classrooms today, indicate that many resonate with Thoreau's celebration of simplicity, and long to retreat to the woods for the sake of their emotional wellbeing. Not everyone can just move into the woods for a few years like Thoreau could, but many would jump at the opportunity were it presented to them.*

But while Thoreau's work suggests the positive effects one's environment can have on one's emotional wellbeing, evidence from the social sciences suggests that one's surroundings can also do emotional harm.

*Sometimes called "winter blues," seasonal affective disorder (SAD), is a form of depression that occurs in otherwise emotionally healthy people during the winter months. Many people dread winter's cold, short days, but for some people, the winter environment inflicts a clinically diagnosable psychological condition. SAD is quite **prevalent**: the demand for treatment options is so large that I first heard about the disorder in an advertisement that played during prime time television.*

In conclusion, there is strong evidence that a large number of people feel emotional effects from their environment. Many are drawn to Thoreau's work because of the appeal of a simple, and nature-filled life, and others are susceptible to the onset of serious depression when the environment becomes harsh in winter.

A note on compliance

The brainstorming and outlining process is meant to help you organize your thoughts, but you don't just turn your brain off when you start writing, so new ideas will occur to you. It's OK to disobey your own outline if you think of something brilliant, but if you completely ignore your plan and just write whatever occurs to you, then you're probably going to end up with a disorganized essay—exactly what you were trying to avoid by outlining in the first place.

Scan

You might not have time for this, and that's OK, but if you finish your essay early, there are a few productive things you can do that don't involve wholesale changes (which are not realistically advisable given the fact that you're writing in pencil). The minute you write the last period on your conclusion, go back to the beginning and **scour** your essay for two things:

1. Grammar errors, especially in the introduction, where they'll really make a bad first impression
2. Opportunities to erase one word and replace it with a better vocabulary word

You'll never know for sure, of course, but the tiny changes you make here might improve how your Essay Star looks on two of its five points, and therefore might tip the scales in your favor if a reader is on the fence about your score.

Process summary

This all might seem a bit **discursive**, but I promise you can get better at it with practice. The following page contains a quick summary of the process.

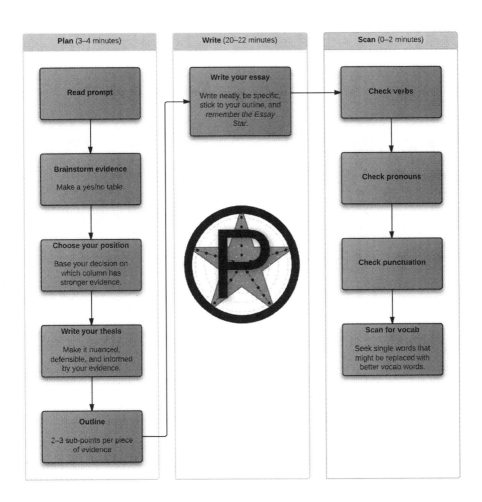

Plan (3–4 minutes)

Read prompt

Brainstorm evidence
Make a yes/no table.

Choose your position
Base your decision on which column has stronger evidence.

Write your thesis
Make it nuanced, defensible, and informed by your evidence.

Outline
2–3 sub-points per piece of evidence

Write (20–22 minutes)

Write your essay
Write neatly, be specific, stick to your outline, and remember the Essay Star.

Scan (0–2 minutes)

Check verbs

Check pronouns

Check punctuation

Scan for vocab
Seek single words that might be replaced with better vocab words.

5. The DOs and DON'Ts of essay writing

In this chapter, I present some common pitfalls I've noticed in students' writing, and (when possible) contrast them with techniques that the best essay writers use. Most of these have already been mentioned in passing earlier on in the book, but I wanted to repeat them here, because they're worth repeating. I see you rereading this chapter the night before the test like it's a beautiful bedtime story.

If you recognize any of your own **suboptimal** habits as you **peruse** the DON'Ts, pay special attention to the DOs—often, bad habits can be replaced with good ones.

Let me just also say this: I'm calling these DOs and DON'Ts, but I'm well aware that some who disobey this advice still write to great effect. I'm not saying there's no place for hypotheticals in good writing, nor am I denying that some **seminal** works contain rhetorical questions. I am simply saying that not all writing practices are equally suitable for all venues. There are times when it might be appropriate to wax philosophical about the essential nature of the universe, but the SAT is not one of them.

Let's do this.

DON'T argue both sides

I'm being a bit controversial by calling this a pitfall at all. Some tutors and writing coaches actually encourage this, insisting that doing so strengthens essays. I respectfully disagree. Taking both sides of an argument is one of the easiest ways to hurt yourself in the "development and support of point of view" department. If you argue both sides of an issue, you confuse your reader (who, remember, is making a quick holistic assessment of your essay) about which side you're actually taking.

It's true that good writers will often analyze the position they disagree with before arguing against it. This kind of writing, in fact, is incredibly common in SAT critical reading passages. Often, the authors of those passages take up more space spelling out the stuff they don't believe than they use to tell you what they do believe. But the SAT essay consists of two handwritten pages, and it must be completed in twenty-five minutes. There's not enough time or space to give both sides of an argument a fair shake.

Time and again, when I see students try to take both sides, they either oversimplify the side they're against so much that it's insulting to the reader, or worse, they spend so much time spelling out the counterargument that they don't have time or space to effectively argue their own position—an epic fail.

DO take nuanced, defensible positions

I understand that SAT essay prompts are often constructed in such a way that it's hard *not* to take both sides. For example, a prompt that asks whether it's important to always tell the truth might be equally well answered in the positive or the negative. Rather than arguing both sides broadly, though, take a nuanced, defensible position that **obviates** the need. In other words, don't spend half your time explaining that telling the truth is good, and then discuss a bunch of instances in which lying would be advisable. Make it clear, right in your thesis, that you're not an **absolutist**, but that you nonetheless value the truth:

Assignment: Is it ever better to lie than to tell the truth?

> *Although circumstances exist in which uncompromising honesty is not the best policy, it is still generally true that it is better to be truthful than it is to lie.*

This is really important, so I'd like to dig deeper here. Imagine a prompt that asks you the frustratingly broad question of whether technology is a **boon** or a **bane** to humanity. Since you're a thoughtful person, you can probably think of instances that would support both broad positions, and you might, as a result, struggle to pick a side, aware of the arguments the other side could make against you. This is why so many people **succumb** to the pitfall of arguing both sides.

Good writers don't let the prompt lure them into **precarious** positions. Rather, they focus narrowly on an aspect of the prompt that allows them to take a strong position. When you're confident in your thesis, you'll spend less energy worrying about fending off obvious rebuttals to your argument and more energy making a strong case.

Assignment: Can technological advances that make life easier have negative consequences?

> *In the grand scheme of things, technological advances improve the human experience, but many technological advances have unintended negative consequences. For example, many teachers blame cellular phones for a host of problems in the classroom, and the overwhelming majority of environmental scientists blame greenhouse gas emissions generated by so many of our modern conveniences for the climate change that endangers us all.*

*There are many obvious benefits to the rapid **proliferation** of cellular phone technology, but a strong case can be made that cellular devices have **exacerbated** age-old challenges in one important area of our culture: education. Teachers are commonly driven to extreme measures to **curtail** phone usage in the classroom, because it causes problems ranging from relatively **benign** student distraction to more pernicious academic dishonesty. Students have always found ways to distract themselves, and some have always tried to cheat, but many educators argue that these problems are worse now than they have ever been in the past, and that cell phones are to blame. My mother is a teacher, and told me recently about a national survey of teachers that ranked cell phone usage in the classroom in the top 3 problems teachers in America face.*

It is difficult to overstate the general comfort and convenience most Americans enjoy relative to our counterparts 100 years ago, but ironically the ways these conveniences are produced pose a grave threat to us all. We are cool in the summer and warm in the winter. We can illuminate dark rooms with the flick of a switch, and we can communicate with our friends across the world in real time, or fly through the air at amazing speeds to visit them in person. Our ancestors would be speechless to see the way we live. But these technological marvels result in the emission of greenhouse gasses, which are warming our planet at an alarming rate. Ice caps are melting, oceans are rising, and severe weather events are becoming more frequent and more dangerous. These facts are a very scary example of the unintended negative consequences that technological advances can have.

*Technology aims to improve the human experience, and for the most part it does. However, it is **naïve** to believe that technology advances do not sometimes also have undesirable effects.*

First of all, note how the sample essay above follows the general structure I've advocated for all along. It's got a nice, short introduction that starts right off with thesis statement. The body paragraphs hit all the main targets of a body paragraph (mini-thesis, concrete evidence). And the conclusion is short.

Now note how both the main thesis and the mini-thesis disarm an obvious criticism right off the bat before focusing narrowly. In the main thesis, the narrow focus is unintended consequences; in the first mini-thesis, the focus is education. Safe in the knowledge that no reader will be thinking, "Yeah but what about cell phones empowering rural farmers in Africa?" as she reads the first body paragraph, the writer can get down to business focusing on the effects of cell phones in classrooms.

A few more thoughts about this technique: First, it takes some practice—if your position is *too* narrow, you'll have a hard time filling two pages with your argument. Second, recognize how this is not the same as the common pitfall of arguing both sides. When you take nuanced, defensible positions, you avoid the temptation to argue both sides by disarming **detractors** in the very beginning. Essentially, you're saying: "Yeah, you probably have some good general points, but I want to speak very specifically about *this*."

DON'T oversell yourself

Imagine you're at a new pizza place that just opened up in town, and the pizza is **serviceable**, but not mind-blowing. Pizza is still pizza, so you're not miserable. If the atmosphere is to your liking you'll probably walk out feeling pretty good, even if the pizza isn't the best you've ever had. Now imagine that the restaurant had a big neon sign out front that claiming that you'd find the "World's Best Pizza" inside. With your expectations set so high, that same middle-of-the-road pizza tastes horrible, and you walk out feeling ripped off. That's the danger of overselling.

Avoid this by not using words your essay can't back up. Don't claim to have *proven* anything. Don't say, "these facts unquestionably demonstrate," or anything like that if, as is true about every SAT essay prompt, a reasonable person could disagree with your position. Don't call a 4-paragraph essay careful or thorough analysis. It takes more than twenty-five minutes and two handwritten pages to give careful analysis.

DON'T philosophize

There's enormous temptation to begin an SAT essay—or any essay, really—with a sweeping **banality** about life, the universe, and everything. But if you fall prey to this temptation, then you're doing what's known as philosophizing, and you're doing yourself a disservice. Philosophizing is a pretty good way to lose your way and hurt yourself in the "organization and focus" point of the Essay Star, and it's why I am so **adamant** that you get right into your thesis statement at the beginning of your essay.

> Don't ever begin an essay with a phrase like "In life," "As humans," or "In a world." Just get right to the point. Your graders will thank you (with higher scores).

Assignment: Is it ever better to lie than to tell the truth?

> *In this life, it is important for we humans to remember to treat each other with respect. One way in which we can show respect for each other is by giving true representations of ourselves in our interactions. The best way to achieve this is to always be honest.*

The only way philosophizing works is when it's read out loud in a voice like you hear in movie trailers. Try it: "In a world..." Cool, right? But you don't get to read your essay out loud to your grader. What the writer of the paragraph above seems to want to say is that honesty is important, but he doesn't just come right out and say it. First he tries to access some deep, fundamental truth about humanity. But do you feel like you know more about the human condition than you did before you read it? No? Neither will your reader. Don't bother.

DO get to (and stick to) the point

I've said it before, but it's worth repeating: The first sentence of your introduction should be your thesis statement, and each body paragraph should begin with a mini-thesis. On the SAT essay, you have two pages and twenty-five minutes to make your argument. There's neither time nor space to **ruminate** on concepts not **germane** to your argument, so you should avoid being wordy at all costs. You should strive to express your ideas with maximum **economy**. To paraphrase the **inimitable** Strunk & White,[20] each word should *tell*.

You make getting and sticking to the point easier for yourself by crafting your thesis statement with **sedulous** care. In spelling out a narrow, nuanced thesis, you make it much easier for yourself not to stray off topic, or to philosophize for a few sentences until you figure out what you really want to say.

Assignment: Can a person's bad deeds make his or her good deeds irrelevant?

Decent: *One example of a person whose accomplishments have been overshadowed by his evil deeds is Genghis Khan, founder of the Mongol Empire. Genghis Khan came from a large family—he had three brothers, one sister, and two half-brothers. Legend has it that he was born with a blood clot in his fist, which was a traditional sign that he was destined to become a great leader. He came to power by uniting many of the nomadic tribes of northeast Asia. As an emperor,*

---

[20] http://en.wikipedia.org/wiki/The_Elements_of_Style

he was responsible for unifying his empire behind a single writing script, which enabled increased communication throughout the region. He was also a champion of religious tolerance—a rarity in his time. Despite these notable accomplishments, Genghis Khan is better known as a brutal warlord, who mercilessly slaughtered whole populations in his conquests. After his death, Genghis Khan's empire was divided into territories and split among his sons. His name will forever be synonymous not with making great strides in early communication and religious tolerance, but rather with fear and bloodshed.

Note that although the paragraph above isn't terrible, it does stray once or twice from the point that the accomplishments of Genghis Khan[21] are overshadowed by his **infamous** brutality. Specifically, information about his siblings isn't really important, nor is the bit at the end about his sons inheriting his empire after his death. Note how much more crisp it feels with its distractions removed.

Assignment: Can a person's bad deeds make his or her good deeds irrelevant?

Better: *One example of a person whose accomplishments have been overshadowed by his evil deeds is Genghis Khan, founder of the Mongol Empire. Legend has it that he was born with a blood clot in his fist, which was a traditional sign that he was destined to become a great leader. Genghis Khan came to power by uniting many of the nomadic tribes of northeast Asia. As an emperor, he was responsible for unifying his empire behind a single writing script, which enabled increased communication throughout the region. He was also a champion of religious tolerance—a rarity in his time. Despite these notable*

---

[21] http://en.wikipedia.org/wiki/Genghis_Khan

accomplishments, Genghis Khan is better known as a brutal warlord, who mercilessly slaughtered whole populations in his conquests. His name will forever be synonymous not with making great strides in early communication and religious tolerance, but rather with fear and bloodshed.

DON'T make stuff up (if you can help it)

OK, look. It's true that nobody fact-checks your work, and it's true that some people do achieve high essay scores with made-up evidence. If you're completely at a loss for a single concrete example, you might have to **fabricate** something as a last resort. But if you approach the SAT essay planning to make up entire events or works of literature out of whole cloth, you're setting yourself up for mediocrity.

I have worked with countless students who have invented books, uncles, and best friends to make their arguments on the SAT essay. It is almost always immediately obvious to me that they're doing it. And although I don't let the fact that I know they're false influence my scoring, the fact of the matter is that made up examples are usually so simplistic that they don't provide enough grist for the analytical mill. If the "support" part of your "development and support of point of view" is shallow and **trite**, you're not going to be achieving a top score. You're just not. In other words, you won't be penalized for the *act* of making something up; you'll be penalized for the poor quality of the evidence you make up.

One of the reasons historical events and good literature make for ideal evidence is that they're complex and multifaceted, so you can write about them at length and with some depth. It's hard to do that about your cousin Steve who failed a chemistry test he didn't study for but then he studied really hard for the next test and aced it.

It's not that you're not *allowed* to make stuff up. It's just that you're probably not very good at it.

DON'T make unsupported claims

Sometimes I see essays that just say the same thing over and over again in slightly different ways, or make a bunch of related claims without offering any real support for them. This is bad writing, and it'll result in mediocre essay scores. Make sure you can support any claim you make with concrete evidence. If you can't support it, don't claim it.

Assignment: Can technological advances that make life easier have negative consequences?

> Bad: *The most important technological innovation happens in the medical field. When people are sick, they are unhappy. Without innovation in medicine, our quality of life would be worse, which would make it impossible for innovation to occur in other fields.*

Do you see how the main claim here, that medical innovation is the most important kind of innovation, is supported by **subordinate** claims, rather than evidence? When the writer says people who are sick are unhappy, that's a claim that needs support. When she says quality of life would be worse without medical innovation, that's a claim too! Let's try that again with some evidence:

Assignment: Can technological advances that make life easier have negative consequences?

> Good: *The most important technological innovation happens in the medical field. Every day, researchers around the world make slow, steady progress towards* **mitigating** *some of society's greatest challenges including HIV/AIDS, cancer, and aging populations. On the TV news last night, I saw an interview with a spokesman from the Center for Disease Control who said that young people today will probably not have to worry about cancer by the time they are old! Freedom*

from the effects of devastating diseases (and worrying about those diseases) will free up future generations of innovators to focus even more on other societal problems. In this way, medical innovation can be a long-term driver of innovation in other fields.

DO be specific

Seriously, it's almost impossible to be too specific in your SAT essay, as long as the details you're citing support your argument. Here's a paragraph about Strom Thurmond:

Assignment: Is it important to remain true to one's convictions?

> Decent: *Longtime US Senator Strom Thurmond's legacy will forever be* **marred** *by his strong opposition to civil rights. He was from the south, and took many positions, like his support of racial segregation, that would be considered* **abhorrent** *by many today. Although he* **moderated** *some of his most controversial positions later in his life, he never apologized or completely reversed them. Senator Thurmond's* **vehement adherence** *to unjust and* **repugnant** *positions have condemned him to a villain's role in the* **annals** *of history, and show the danger of holding beliefs too firmly.*

That's not too bad, right? There's some good sentence structure in there, and a bunch of appropriately used vocabulary words. But note the lack of specifics! Do you get the impression this person really knows very much about Strom Thurmond? Compare that paragraph to this one, with some specifics in gray:

Assignment: Is it important to remain true to one's convictions?

> Better and more specific: *Strom Thurmond represented South Carolina in the US Senate for 49 years, but he is*

*best known (and most **reviled**) for his vehement opposition to civil rights. In 1948, before he was elected to the Senate, he ran for president as a segregationist—an unquestionably **abhorrent** position today—and won less than 3% of the popular vote. Undeterred by the unpopularity of his position, he persisted in opposition of social progress. He holds the record for longest filibuster by a single senator, which he set when he spoke in opposition to the Civil Rights Act of 1957 for longer than 24 hours. Although he **moderated** his position on race later in his life, he failed to convince his many **detractors** by continuing to defend his segregationist positions on the **dubious** basis of states' rights. Senator Thurmond's unjust and **repugnant** positions have condemned him to a villain's role in the annals of history, and show the danger of holding beliefs too firmly.*

DON'T get bogged down in unnecessary summary

Every detail you include about a piece of evidence should serve to further your argument. If you're using George Washington's honesty about the cherry tree to argue for truthfulness in general, it matters that Washington was the first President of the United States because that suggests that the way he lived his life might have led to great success. It *doesn't* matter that his wife was named Martha, or that he had wooden teeth, or that he killed his sensei in a duel and never said why.

DON'T use the same example twice

Sometimes it's pretty tough not to do this, so you shouldn't panic if you have to, but if you can avoid using super-parallel examples—like Gandhi and Martin Luther King Jr., *who was inspired by Gandhi to pursue nonviolent protest*—you should. Try to make your argument multi-dimensional. In other words…

DO argue the same point from different angles

The most convincing arguments make the same point from multiple angles. If you're able to show, for example, that doing *X* leads to a desirable result *Y*, and also show that *not* doing *X* leads to an undesirable result, *not Y*, then you've made a more compelling argument than someone who just had multiple examples of doing *X* and therefore achieving *Y*. I'm being vague. Let me illustrate:

Assignment:	Is the ability to overcome personal obstacles more important than raw talent in determining a person's success?

Decent: *People who are able to weather personal difficulties are more likely to achieve success in the long run. In his memoir, <u>Wherever I Wind Up</u>, Knuckleballer R.A. Dickey, who won the National League Cy Young Award in 2012, explains how he* **persevered** *despite a long list of devastating setbacks before achieving major league success. Similarly, my father was fired from ten different jobs before he got a job at his current company, and worked his way up to the position of vice president.*

Better: *People who are able to weather personal difficulties are more likely to achieve success in the long run. In his memoir, <u>Wherever I Wind Up</u>, Knuckleballer R.A. Dickey, who won the National League Cy Young Award in 2012, explains how he persevered despite a long list of devastating setbacks before achieving major league success. Unlike R.A. Dickey, my friend Darren, widely considered the best athlete in our school, ruined his chances at a college football scholarship when he quit the team after the coach benched him for missing practice.*

See what's going on here? In the first example, the writer basically uses the same example twice. R.A. Dickey and the writer's father are different people, but their experiences play out roughly the same storyline: they endure some tough times, and then find success. In the second example, the writer's friend Darren provides a nice contrast to Dickey, by illustrating that people who *don't* deal well with personal difficulties can end up missing opportunities.

DON'T rely on hypothetical arguments

A hypothetical argument is one that's based not on concrete evidence, but on **conjecture** and opinion instead. It's a bad idea to use an argument like this because you don't know your audience, and you assume they'll agree with your assessment of a made-up situation at your peril. Here's an example of a hypothetical argument:

Assignment: Can technological advances that make life easier have negative consequences?

> *Technology is important to our daily lives. If a person woke up one day and found out that all her electronics had been taken away, she wouldn't know what to do with herself. Everything would take too long, she would forget all her appointments, and her friends would be annoyed that she wasn't returning their texts. Without technology, we cannot function in today's society.*

What's so bad about that? Well, what if the grader who reads it is a wilderness buff who hates the fact that he has to hear people talking on their cell phones everywhere he goes, and wishes we could return to a time before texting? Believe it or not, people like that exist. This example is unconvincing because there are no facts the reader has to agree with, only interpretations of a fictional scenario with which he may or may not agree.

When you use concrete examples, you give yourself the opportunity to get on the same page with your grader—the facts are the facts.

Once you're on common ground, you've got a better chance at convincing your grader that your analysis of the facts is solid. When you use a hypothetical example, you risk having your grader disagree with the basic premises of your argument. If that happens, he's not going to be very likely to agree with your conclusion.

DON'T ask rhetorical questions

It's a bad idea to ask rhetorical questions for much the same reason it's a bad idea to use hypotheticals. When you don't know your audience, a rhetorical question (unless it's a *really* good one) has a pretty high probability of landing with a thud. If your reader is following your argument, a rhetorical question is an annoying cliché that he or she is awfully sick of seeing in SAT essays. If he or she is *not* following your example, it's even worse—a reminder that your essay is unconvincing, and an acknowledgement on your part that you think you're being *very* convincing. You don't want to make your reader think poorly of you, do you? (See what I did there.)

DON'T use clichés

Most of the issues I've seen involving clichés come at the beginning of an essay. Students try to begin their essay with a bit of style by using an old saying they know that seems relevant to the prompt. When I read openings like this, I cringe. If something really is an old popular saying (e.g. "whoever smelt it dealt it") then it occurred to you at just about the same time it occurred to tens of thousands of other kids writing on the same prompt as you. Imagine you're a grader and student after student cites the same tired **apothegm**. It'd drive you *nuts*.

Don't drive your graders nuts. Skip the **maxim**, and get right into your thesis and argument.

DON'T get too fancy with the vocabulary

This is a subtle point, but there's a fine line between exhibiting your ability to use big words and showboating your prodigious personal lexicon. Write naturally, the way someone might talk. Here's an analogy for you: vocabulary : writer :: spice : chef. Three or four big words sprinkled into an entire essay is enough. Too much **highfalutin** vocabulary can get pretty obnoxious, just like too much spice can ruin a good dish.

6. Bringing it all together

So that's about it. Seriously. If you're able to incorporate all the advice from the previous chapters into your writing process on test day, you'll be in great shape.

The remainder of this book will contain real essays submitted to me by students, followed by an Essay Star, a score, and my comments. I hope, through these examples, to cement the advice spelled out in this book up to this point.

Greed is good?

> Greed, for lack of a better word, is good. Greed is right. Greed works. Greed clarifies, cuts through, and captures, the essence of the evolutionary spirit. Greed, in all of its forms—greed for life, for money, for love, knowledge—has marked the upward surge of mankind and greed, you mark my words, will not only save Teldar Paper, but that other malfunctioning corporation called the U.S.A.
>
> Adapted from Oliver Stone and Stanley Weiser, *Wall Street*

Assignment: Can acting in one's own self-interest make the world a better place? Plan and write an essay in which you develop your point of view on this issue. Support your position with reasoning and examples taken from your reading, studies, experience, or observations.

Sample essay 1.1

Greed is definitely important, because it is the upmost necessity for self improvement. For growing in life, greed is must. Greed is needed for ambitions, to look for opportunities, and to set our goals. Greed makes a man feel lack of something he might want to have in his life and in this process, he starts searching for ways, and hardworking to achieve it. Being taken on a positive way, greed proves to be the most important aspect for a man's growth in life.

On the other hand, greed can even lead to destruction of one's life if directed in a wrong way. It is rightly said that greed works, but only when the negative aspects of greed are eliminated. Greed is good only till one does not destroy himself, others, his family, society or culture in order to gain something without making efforts for it. Greed in a way to snatch something out is not appropriate. Greed in someone who is not ready to work, can harm him, as well as even make him harm others, just to fulfill the greed. Such greed ends in people becoming thieves and robbers who take the wrong path, just to fulfill their greeds.

Greed should just be used as a motivation to improve oneself on an individual level. Greed helps in developing new ideas and new ways to achieve our goals. It leads to planning and organizing ourselves in order to make ourselves the way it is needed to match our wants. Greed directly affects one's self interests, and point of views about something.

Looking at someone having something you might want, makes you feel greedy, and sometimes jealous. This jealousy, and greed makes one try his best to gain what he wants. In this way, he improves himself and his life. In totality, he improves the world.

It is absolutely true that greed leads to prosperity in life and acting on one's own self-interest can make this world a better place. A man is a small part or say a piece of this world, and if slowly, each and every piece tries to improve itself, it will lead to a great puzzle, the world. Also, by making his own life better, a man will improve his surroundings and the society and will set a culture for the next generation.

The river is made up of tiny drops, so if each drop is purified, it is certain that the river will be the most pure. Similarly, if each individual gets greedy, he will try to purify himself, his life and the world around him, henceforth purifying the world and making it a better place to live in.

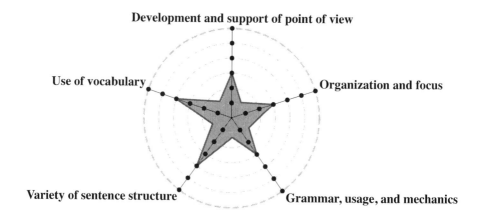

As you read this essay, some things probably jumped out at you right away. There's a bit of misused vocabulary—"hardworking" is an adjective, but it's used as a verb in this essay, and I don't think "greeds" is a word. The sentence structure is pretty repetitive, too: about half the sentences begin with the word "greed."

Those are major weaknesses, but I want to dig deeper. Another big problem with this essay is that it's more of a meditation on the different things greed can mean than it is an argument that addresses the question in the prompt. In other words, it's mostly philosophizing. To the extent that it *does* address the prompt, it says greed is both good and bad.

Finally, note the claims that are made and then go unsupported. For example, "It is absolutely true that greed leads to prosperity in life and acting on one's own self-interest can make this world a better place." *HOW?!* In support of this claim there is only a metaphor about a puzzle (vague) and then a repetition of the claim: "Also, by making his own life better, a man will improve his surroundings and the society and will set a culture for the next generation." This essay's graders will likely have counterexamples in mind almost immediately. For instance, a grader might be thinking that in the recent financial crisis, greed led a few men to make their lives better to the great **detriment** of society as a whole.

While I can imagine a grader giving this essay a 4, I think it's most likely to get it a 3s. Still, in cases where it's not obvious, I like to hedge my bets, so I gave it one of each.

Sample essay 1.2

Acting in one's own self-interest can indeed make the world a better place. Greed, through cause and effect, can be turned from a self-profit situation to an integral shift in the lives of many.

At the dawn of the Industrial Revolution in America, one specific businessman led the automobile industry. This man was Henry Ford, who introduced commercial automobiles, a mode of transportation that allowed anyone to ride in style. Ford's main interest was to make a profit, just like any other businessman. Not only was Ford's innovation a result of acting out of his own self interest, but it also changed the world into a more modern, connected place. His greed, his quest to make money, was incredible change that most definitely made the world a better place.

As for me, I have seen small-scale implications of this theory. During my freshman and sophomore years of high school, I completed community service hours here and there, knowing I would need service hours for National Honor Society membership and college applications. At first, I was acting out of complete and utter self-interest. Over time, however, I learned how my work in the community really affected the lives of others. Now, I jump at nearly every opportunity to do community service. Even a couple hours can change one person's world, and acting in my own self-interest was the only way that I was able to see how a single person, like myself, could make my community a better place.

Both of these examples show instances of greed which turned into a positive influence on the world. They support the idea that greed, no matter how grotesque a word it may be, can be a good thing. Where would we be without the family car or community volunteers? Without acting out of self-interest, we would not be living in the progressive, modern world that we know today.

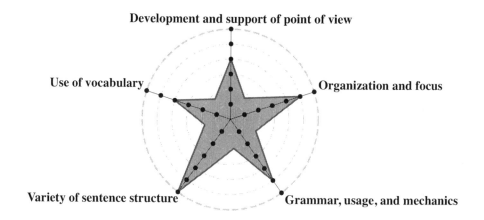

Development and support of point of view

Use of vocabulary

Organization and focus

Variety of sentence structure

Grammar, usage, and mechanics

This is a pretty solid essay, but there's room for improvement. The writer employs nicely varied sentence structure. The vocabulary isn't bad, it's also not great—the word **grotesque**, which means **incongruous**, or unnaturally distorted, is used incorrectly in describing the word greed. Although it's generally free of grammar and usage errors, there's some pretty awkward phrasing right in the intro: "Greed, through cause and effect, can be turned from a self-profit situation to an integral shift in the lives of many." Huh?

This essay's weakest point, though, is that its first example isn't well supported. Henry Ford [22] was a businessman, yes, but are all businessmen necessarily greedy? Is greed the same as wanting to make money? This essay seems to make that claim. If I don't believe he was greedy, it doesn't matter if I agree that Ford's innovation was beneficial to the world. I'm not convinced that greed was responsible for that innovation.

The essay is also pretty short on specifics. What was Ford's great innovation, really? Why not mention that he popularized the assembly line? And we're not just missing details about Ford. What kind of community service does our writer do? What, specifically, led the

[22] http://en.wikipedia.org/wiki/Henry_Ford

writer to see community service in a new light? I want details! I want to read about how you volunteered at a hospital and forged a deep friendship with a World War II veteran who told incredible stories and instilled in you a sense of duty to serve your country!

Sample essay 1.3

Although greed can be a vice, it is ultimately and inherently necessary in a free-market enterprise such as the one we have in America. Greed can cause problems, but if the power of greed is harnessed for good, the possibilities that come from the opportunities brought out by greed are immense. Greed, along with fear and love, is among the greatest motivational emotions known to man and healthy greed is beneficial to not just oneself but to those around him or her.

One paradigm in which this case is abundantly clear is in the life and philanthropic works of one of the world's richest men Warren Buffett. This stock market and business mogul dominated the free market in America to make his fortune. His greed for power, success, and subsequently wealth was one of the largest factors in his meteoric rise to power to financial gain. Buffett, however, also saw the destructive power that greed could have. He knew that greed could destroy him much faster than it had helped build him up. This is a "healthy greed," which means that he uses it as motivation but does not let it consume him. Buffett had originally acted in his own self-interest, but through his accumulation of wealth and resources he has helped thousands of people. His impact, however, is not just in monetary value because the jobs and companies that he has helped create number in the thousands. Buffett truly made the world a better place through his selfish greed.

Another paradigm in which selfish motives and greed has helped people is in the actions of John L. Lewis. This talented investment banker was the epitome of a stock market banker filled with greed. Through his self-interest he had made a fortune, but he wanted more.

Consequently, in the stock market crash of 2008, the start the "Great Recession," he lost nearly everything. He had attempted to double his portfolio and ended up losing. Lewis, however, learned from his mistake and he has since gained much of his wealth back. He is also now an advisor to many young stock market evaluators. The countless young men and women that he is educating on the dangers of greed are benefitting from Lewis. He learned from the greed and his self-interest and proceeded to help others. Greed had made Lewis and greed had broken Lewis, but he learned and has helped people through what he has learned from his own greed and self-interest.

Greed is a characteristic that young children are taught to avoid. Fables and folklore include a plethora of paradigms and anecdotes to illustrate to young children that greed is a terrible vice, but those children's stories do not tell the full story. They leave out the fact that greed drives people to do more, work harder, and outlast the competition. Greed runs the economy and the world. Without it, people would not strive to be better than others. Learning to harness the power of greed and acting in self-interest can and often does make the world a better place.

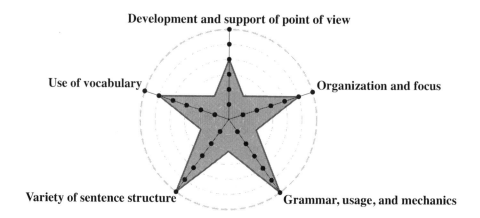

The grammar and variety of sentence structure in this essay are quite good. The vocabulary is mostly fine, although the two uses of **paradigm** as a fancy word for "example" are a bit extreme. The essay's major weakness is that its point of view seems to become a bit muddled as the essay develops.

The thesis seems to be that greed can be bad, but it makes the world go 'round, so can also be good. This is a bit confusing, and is going to make it hard for the writer to make a strong point. And indeed, that bears out. Both body paragraphs basically have the same structure: some guy was greedy, realized that being purely greedy was bad, and then became better by being philanthropic. Perhaps the current thesis could be replaced with the assertion that greed itself is bad, but some people are both greedy and philanthropic, and *that combination* can be a good thing.

Here's a passage from the essay that I think exemplifies its main shortcoming:

> Buffett, however, also saw the destructive power that
> greed could have. He knew that greed could destroy
> him much faster than it had helped build him up. This is
> a "healthy greed," which means that he uses it as

motivation but does not let it consume him. Buffett had originally acted in his own self-interest, but through his accumulation of wealth and resources he has helped thousands of people. His impact, however, is not just in monetary value because the jobs and companies that he has helped create number in the thousands. Buffett truly made a world a better place through his selfish greed.

That's not particularly well organized, but it also has me scratching my head as to the writer's true position. Greed has destructive power? But people should be greedy? What does "healthy greed" really mean? Why create and define the term only to use it once? Was it the greed of Warren Buffett[23] that made the world a better place, or did he improve the world *in spite* of his greed?

Another issue that's preventing this from achieving a top score is that the two pieces of evidence are remarkably similar—a common symptom of fabrication disease. There have been a few men named John L. Lewis in history, but if there's a prominent Wall Street character by that name, Wikipedia hasn't heard of him. Again, graders are never going to look up someone you write about to see if he's a real person, but that doesn't mean making up examples won't hurt you, because *it's really hard to make up good examples.* This essay is weakened not because John L. Lewis isn't a real investment banker, but because his story doesn't add much to the development of the author's point of view. If this writer had spent a bit more time outlining and developing his thesis before he began writing, he might have planned for more diversity in his examples.

All that said, this essay was clearly written by a strong writer—one who is capable of a top score. By being more careful in picking a nuanced, easily defensible thesis in future essays, he'll make it much easier not to fall into these same traps.

---

[23] http://en.wikipedia.org/wiki/Warren_Buffett

Sample essay 1.4

In an age dominated by technology, entertainment and materialism, greed cannot be avoided. To put it best, greed is a virus. Although not every member of our society is infected, it only takes a few people to nurture and foster our inherent feelings of greed before it spreads to others and poisons society. Consequently, as we embrace greed, we become superficial and so engaged with self-indulgence that we become disillusioned and apathetic to the worsening global crises around us, leading to the degradation rather that the betterment of our society.

The rise of consumerism is by far the prime cause of the ever-increasing presence of greed and self-indulgence in our society. The media and the entertainment industry through advertisements and product placement brainwash our culture into desiring the latest Apple products and fashion trends as reality TV and sitcoms continue to drown us in triviality. As a result, programs such as documentaries and news programs that educate the public and foster awareness are overshadowed. This triviality and materialism lays the foundation for creating a generation not only dominated by greed but also disillusioned into believing apathy is acceptable, both of which cause bright young minds to act in self-interest rather than harnessing the tools we have to better society. If we are not careful, we will end up so self-absorbed that our society will evolve into a dystopia such as the one presented by Ray Bradbury in Fahrenheit 451 where books are burned and families are replaced by TV and radio shows.

Many people would argue, however, that self-interest and greed are not detrimental to society. Millionaires, especially those which are philanthropists, believe that with self-interest, we in fact encourage individuals to invest and build up their self-worth which that in turn alleviate our global economic crisis by creating a stable economy based on healthy competition and confident investment. In addition, the new wealth would allow people to allocate more of their money to charities and programs that indirectly contribute to a better society.

However, these people are victims of disillusionment. The reality is only a few wealthy people such as Bill Gates can help better society their seemingly endless amount of money. While these can have impact on the short term and immediate crises in our society, in the long term, we cannot hope to solve all of our problems by merely throwing money at the problem. Instead, we must educate our society so that individuals are not only aware of the problems but also so that we can harness tools such as social networking to unify us and provide solutions to problems such as global warming and the spread of AIDS in destitute countries.

Score: 10

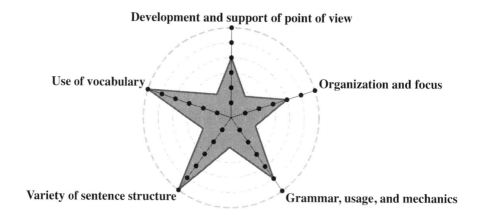

Development and support of point of view

Use of vocabulary

Organization and focus

Variety of sentence structure

Grammar, usage, and mechanics

The writer displays an impressively developed comfort with the English language in this essay. Her sentence structure is varied— there's a nice rhythm to her prose. Her use of advanced vocabulary is appropriate and doesn't feel forced. Grammatically, the essay is *pretty* good, but there's a little room for improvement. Let's have a look at a sentence:

> *"This triviality and materialism lays the foundation for creating a generation not only dominated by greed but also disillusioned into believing apathy is acceptable, both of which cause bright young minds to act in self-interest rather than harnessing the tools we have to better society."*

I'd reword that. She's using the singular conjugation of *to lay*, but she's really saying triviality and materialism (two things) lay a foundation. Further, she shifts from talking about bright young minds in the third person to using the first person when she says, "the tools we have." Our writer is clearly a bright young mind herself, but she should avoid switching between third and first person when talking about the same group of people.

Her biggest opportunity for improvement, though, is her argument. The prompt asks whether acting in one's own self-interest can be good. Her argument is, generally, that it cannot, but it takes her a long time to get there and by the time she states her position, she doesn't have much time to support it with evidence. The one example she does include at the end is Bill Gates, who seems to be the counterexample to her claim.

This essay gets a 10, easy. But the writer clearly has a way with words, so I'd say that she could be writing 12s with some increased focus on structure. Her skillful use of language should complement her argument, not supplant it.

Then I'll be all around in the dark

And the great owners, who must lose their land in an upheaval, the great owners with access to history, with eyes to read history and to know the great fact: when property accumulates in too few hands it is taken away. And that companion fact: when a majority of the people are hungry and cold they will take by force what they need. And the little screaming fact that sounds through all history: repression works only to strengthen and knit the repressed.

Adapted from John Steinbeck, *The Grapes of Wrath*

Assignment: Should the needs of the many outweigh the desires of a powerful few? Plan and write an essay in which you develop your point of view on this issue. Support your position with reasoning and examples taken from your reading, studies, experience, or observations.

Sample essay 2.1

The needs of the few should outweigh the needs of the powerful few. The basis of our government is democracy where people have the voice and the fundamental principle is that the power is given to the citizens. Civil rights activists such as Gandhi have proven this to be true. Several examples from past events clearly demonstrate that the needs of the many should outweigh the powerful few.

As demonstrated, in the American Revolution the majority overthrew the powerful few in order to achieve their needs of representation in government. Our founding fathers created a historical document that created a government for the people and by the people, the US Constitution. Prior to the American Revolution colonists didn't have much say in the political process that governed them. For example, neither the Stamp Act of 1750 nor the Tea Act had the presentation of the colonists in mind. Colonists fought for their rights and over time eradicated British control. We soon declared our independence on July 4th, 1776. Ever since then we have been a government for the people and each US Citizen holds basic political rights they can vote, protest, and according to a quote from Benjamin Franklin "It is the citizens reasonability to overthrow the government if it isn't function". By giving the people the voice in the government our country is better able to solve problems and develop legislation that benefits us all.

Through the actions of Mahatma Gandhi it is evident that the needs of the many should outweigh the powerful few. Gandhi fought for over 50 years to achieve the basic rights for everyone in India will aiming to bring democracy to the colony. Gandhi didn't simply want to fight for his rights but rather everyone's rights. On August 15th, 1954 Gandhi finally brought democracy to India. The people of India now had basic rights and could govern themselves. By having the people govern themselves society is more readily able to fix the problems at hand and the general wellbeing of the country improves along with it.

After careful analysis of our Founding Fathers and Gandhi it is indeed true that the needs of the many should outweigh the powerful few. To prevent abuse of power it is important that the majority has a say in the government rather than the powerful minority. As in the case of the American Revolution and the Gandhi's fight for freedom, the powerful few will on do what is in the best interest for them whereas in the majority everyone has equal say and everything is done for the benefit of everyone.

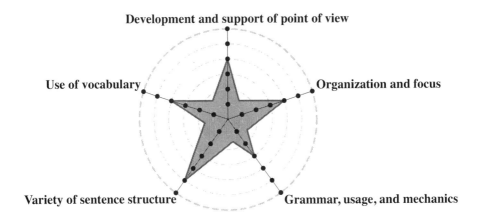

This essay suffers a bit from a lack of editing. Did you notice the mistake in the first sentence? The argument in this essay is about the needs of the many, but the very first sentence gets it twisted and says that the "*needs of the few should outweigh the needs of the powerful few.*" Oops! Of course, if this was the only mistake in the whole essay, it wouldn't be a huge deal, but it puts the reader on alert for more mistakes. I had a professor once who said that typos are like cockroaches—once you see one you're thinking there must be more. In other words, once a reader sees one mistake like that's he's scanning a bit more carefully for errors. Therefore, mistakes in the first sentence are particularly costly: they cause your readers to look more carefully and catch other grammar and usage errors they might otherwise blow right by in their quick read of your essay.

The intro mentions "our government" and Gandhi by name, but then proceeds to claim that "several examples from past events" support the thesis. Once you've specifically mentioned your evidence, there's no need to back up and be vague about them again.

There are a few style issues in the essay. For the American Revolution paragraph alternates between talking about in the third person "colonists," and using first person pronouns like "our" and "we." It's not great to switch back and forth like that. In a historical context, since the writer couldn't possibly have been alive, it's more appropriate to write in the third person.

I want to point out one more **incongruity** here. The intro and conclusion write checks that the essay can't possibly cash. Words like *proven* and *clearly demonstrate* in the intro, and claims about *careful analysis* in the conclusion, are overselling the argument a bit. A careful analysis wouldn't misquote Benjamin Franklin, or gloss over the fact that not everyone was granted the right to vote right away. The Gandhi example works, but again, this essay makes no reference to the peaceful resistance that was a hallmark of Gandhi's campaign for independence. You're not fact checked, but remember that your graders have probably read about Gandhi *thousands* of times. Even if they had never heard of him before they started reading SAT essays, they're experts now. Don't tell them you've provided careful analysis; let them decide for themselves.

Sample essay 2.2

The needs of the many outweigh the needs of the few. The whole premise of government is based on the fact that the needs of the many outweigh the needs of the few. History is rife with examples of times when the people would rise up against the powerful few. From Julius Caesar to Oliver Cromwell, the majority has demonstrated that it has complete power over the whole and it will execute its demands under extreme conditions.

John Locke once stated that we all sign a social contract with our government and they cannot violate the natural rights of the citizens. The majority is the one who has signed the contract and they are the captain of the ship they call government. Once a government violates that system, the majority has an obligation to overthrow and implement a new system that will not take advantage of those rights. While there may be a few in control, their needs do not outweigh the needs of the majority they represent. Looking back even further, Oliver Cromwell was placed in government because the previous rulers abused the natural rights of the citizens.

Oliver Cromwell, like John Locke, is related to the functioning of government. His actions put him in power of a new British kingdom. The monarchy of old was a small, yet powerful group, and their needs were shown to not have as much influence and power as the needs of the majority. After he died, his son tried to resume control; however, the people foresaw this as another opportunity for a monarchy in which the people would have their natural rights abused. The power of monarchy throughout history has shown to corrupt even the most noble of individuals and because of that, people like Julius Caesar are appointed to protect the rights of the many.

Known as the people's fearless leader, Julius Caesar led the Roman Empire to become one of the most prosperous empires of all time. His ascension to emperor started as a triumvirate in which the rights of the majority were protected. Even though he slowly grew into the class of the rich, he continued to be a benevolent ruler. His infamous death shows that the rights of the majority outweigh those of the few because when Caesar grew too powerful, he was murdered. The power of the crown, while greedily taken, is unmercifully lost when pitted against the power of the people.

As history shows, the power and rights of the majority are more powerful than the needs of the few. This trend continues on into the future and as we look to our incoming rulers to guide us, they should be cognizant of this fact.

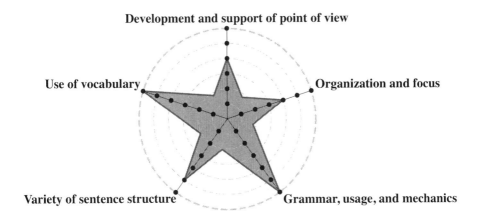

This is a promising essay, but there's still plenty of room for improvement. Vocab and grammar are nice, and so is sentence structure, *mostly*. See how the first paragraph feels a bit repetitive? That's unvaried sentence structure—each of the first three sentences ends with the word "few," and the word "outweigh" is used twice in rapid succession. Not a huge deal, but something to take note of.

The transitions in this essay are misplaced. The first mention of Oliver Cromwell,[24] for example, should come at the beginning of the Cromwell paragraph, not the end of the Locke paragraph. This makes the essay feel less organized than it really is.

I dig the use of John Locke.[25] Note how the essay isn't hurt by a lack of an actual quote from Locke—the writer says what Locke said without feeling the need to fabricate a quote about it. Nice.

The Cromwell paragraph is OK too, although the bit about his son should either be omitted or elaborated upon. This is why I prefer a 4-paragraph essay to a 5-paragraph one—4 paragraphs give you, as a writer, more room for a deep dive into a piece of evidence.

---

[24] http://en.wikipedia.org/wiki/Oliver_Cromwell
[25] http://en.wikipedia.org/wiki/John_locke

The Julius Caesar[26] paragraph is another one that would be better with a bit more development:

> *Known as the people's fearless leader, Julius Caesar*
> *led the Roman Empire to become one of the most*
> *prosperous empires of all time. His ascension to*
> *emperor started as a triumvirate in which the rights of*
> *the majority were protected. Even though he slowly*
> *grew into the class of the rich, he continued to be a*
> *benevolent ruler. His infamous death shows that the*
> *rights of the majority outweigh those of the few*
> *because when Caesar grew too powerful, he was*
> *murdered.*

The beginning of that excerpt is really setting me up to like Caesar—to celebrate him for representing the common people. Then, all of the sudden, he gets too powerful and gets murdered! I want details about *how* he got too powerful. What did he do? Did the people voice their discontent? Why were they unhappy with them? Which of their needs weren't being met? Again, eliminating one paragraph and stretching the other two out a bit might have made this a more convincing essay.

---

[26] http://en.wikipedia.org/wiki/Julius_Caesar

Sample essay 2.3

One need not scour the globe for examples of majority winning; it is simply enough to find examples anywhere one looks. Through repetition, humans have learned that failing to address what the larger population wants does no one any good. As majority will always rule, it is only natural for the needs of many to outweigh the desires of a powerful few.

This can be seen in many incidents throughout history. Taisho Japan, for example, fell victim to such a case. As the economy and government grew increasingly corrupt throughout the 1920s and 1930s, citizens could not help but look elsewhere for the necessary change. The military took over almost immediately, giving rise to prominent militarism. This is only one example of how the majority needed to be heard—since they were not, change was made simply without the consent of the powerful few.

1984 by George Orwell also gets this point through. The oppressed members of a society where big brother was always watching them needed desperately to change their situation. As a result, underground rebel groups formed. While in the end they were shut down, such united dissent should never be ignored. If so many people express the need for freedom, it is simply wrong to ignore them.

This can also be seen in the real world. Protests from the 99% are happening in the US everywhere, a clear indication that members of society are tired of the uneven wealth distribution. Their undying call for reform should overpower those in government, as the united consensus strongly shows the needs of the many need to be addressed. If the majority of the population is unhappy, there is simply no way the powerful few in charge can be left powerful. Clearly the needs of the many should outweigh the desires of the few, even if they are powerful.

With examples from literature, history, and the real world, it is obvious the needs of the many should and do outweigh the desires of a few. Corruption of those in power, whether it is the prime ministers of Japan in the 1920s, the dystopian big brother government, or the uneven wealth distribution prominent in America today, will forever serve as an example of where the citizens' needs should reign over what the powerful few are saying or doing. Without doubt, repression only serves to strengthen those who are repressed; in correlation, the majority will simply grow stronger when left unheard. Thus, the needs of the many should and do outweigh the desires of the powerful few.

Score: 11

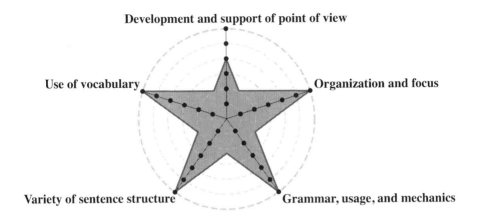

Development and support of point of view
Use of vocabulary
Organization and focus
Variety of sentence structure
Grammar, usage, and mechanics

Not bad! There are three decent pieces of evidence here. This is both a strength and a weakness. It's a strength because it shows that the writer understands the question and is able to develop a point of view quickly based on her studies and her knowledge of the world around her. But it's a weakness because each example leaves me wanting more. Tell me more about Taishō Japan![27] What do you mean the military took over "almost immediately"? Was there a lot of bloodshed? What happened to the leaders in power before the military takeover? What happened after the military takeover? Were the needs of the majority met?

If I were planning this essay, having jotted down a few pieces of evidence I might want to write about, I'd probably decide to omit *1984*, for three related reasons:

1. Tons of people write about *1984*, and it's not *great* for this point since my argument is going to be that the government should not ignore the needs of the people, even though in *1984* it does and gets away with it.
2. I have more interesting things to say about Taishō Japan and the Occupy movement,[28] and

---

[27] http://en.wikipedia.org/wiki/Taish%C5%8D_period
[28] http://en.wikipedia.org/wiki/Occupy_movement

3. Leaving out the *1984* paragraph gives me more room to delve deeper into my other pieces of evidence.

I'd like to see the flourish in the introductory paragraph toned down a bit—I don't think the first sentence makes the right first impression. The rest of the essay is stronger without it. But that's not a huge deal.

I'd also prefer a bit less of an **assertion** of certainty at the end of the essay—"without doubt" is a classing overselling phrase. In two of the three pieces of evidence presented, what our writer thinks *should* happen—that the needs of the majority are met—doesn't happen. In *1984* the rebellion is squashed, and (at the time of this writing) the Occupy movement has gotten a lot of attention, but hasn't exactly overthrown any governments yet. There's a convincing argument to be made that the movement has lost significant steam. A little less **bombast** at the end would have made this essay a bit stronger.

You are where you are

Physically, morally, and emotionally we are woven into the web of life with old-growth redwoods and rainforests and dying lakes and polluted rivers. We need them, not simply as a matter of intelligent resource management, but for the good of our souls. The same toxins that kill them run in our blood, the ugliness of their suffering afflicts our eye, for all we know images of their dire fate haunt our dreams. And surely children who grow into life without knowing wild nature will be less than fully human.

Adapted from Theodore Roszak, "Sanity, the psyche, and the spotted owl"

Assignment: Does one's emotional wellbeing partially depend on one's environment? Plan and write an essay in which you develop your point of view on this issue. Support your position with reasoning and examples taken from your reading, studies, experience, or observations.

Sample essay 3.1

It is a commonly held conviction that one's wellbeing does not change whether one is in the midst of a great forest or in the center of a great metropolis. Such a viewpoint is unfortunately common, for not only is it mistaken and misguided, it is also misleading and egregiously incorrect. Instead, our lives are hopelessly intertwined with nature; in fact, our wellbeing depends on nature. Though the myopic adopt this provincial creed because they believe that we are humans and therefore are able to exist independently of nature, in reality, we are actually inevitable products of our environment and are therefore influenced emotionally by it. Two episodes from history serve as compelling examples of this universal truth.

First of all, closeness to nature may make us feel more attuned to the world. For example, the general Albert Wood was a famous warrior for the Cerarian Army during the early 1900s. At first, when he was born in 1834 to a poor family in the center of the capital Elmore, he was known to be a petulant and irritable man. Once, for instance, he even killed his own dog as a 10-year old because the dog would not learn to steal food from a neighbor. The situation worsened much more at age 18, when his parents died. He was regarded as a man who was constantly picking random arguments even with strangers. This all changed when he first visited a forest at age 21. Breathing in solemn tones of green and brown in the quiet forest, he was not accustomed to the soothing trickling sound of a small creek; no, indeed, he had lived all his life listening to the growl of the industrial machine, the cacophonous clamor of a city marketplace. In the forest, Albert Wood felt much calmer. As a result, he adopted a gentler disposition and became a much more agreeable man; he finally became a general through a series of acquaintances who admired his manner. Albert's manner greatly changed when he was exposed to a different environment, one of forest and nature.

Furthermore, it was no coincidence that my great-grandfather, a man named Joe Steeler, became a famous businessman in the mid-20th century. In his autobiography, he attributed his great success selling shoe-soles not to his friends or to his luck, but to the way he grew up. Whenever he felt empty, irritated, or impetuous as a child, he would follow a certain log road on a nearby mountain. As in Albert's case, the quietness had a palliative effect. Meanwhile, as soon as he went back to his house, he would suddenly become irritable again, until he conjured up in his mind's eye the quiet and gentle noise on the log road. Then, he would take a deep breath and resume his work, reinvigorated and reenergized. Such events contributed greatly to his success; as a shoe-businessman, while his competitors would engage in angry debate, as though influenced by the honking of a car's horn or the mindless prattle in the great city, he himself would be unperturbed by any of the mindless insults aimed at him; he would be unruffled and undisturbed, just like the great redwood or the great sequoias.

In conclusion, our environment contributes greatly to our wellbeing. Nature has a calming effect and can change our disposition greatly, as evidenced by both Woods and my grandfather. Sometimes, I wonder why people do not all revert to living in forests rather than it cities. At least then people will not fight over overwhelmingly petty matters.

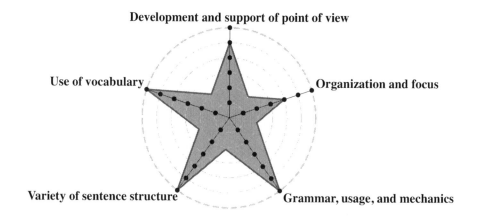

I really agonized over the score for this one, which means it's a great example to include here in this book. First, it's clear this kid can write. The full points granted on vocabulary, variety of sentence structure, and grammar are well deserved. That doesn't mean the essay's perfect on those dimensions, though. I think, for example, it goes way overboard with the vocabulary use in this phrase: "Though the **myopic** adopt this **provincial creed**..." As a result, the sentence, and therefore the whole introductory paragraph, feels a bit muddled.

But the main problem with the intro is that it tries to do way too much. Is it a "commonly held conviction" that people aren't emotionally influenced by their surroundings? A conviction is something people think about often—some of my commonly held convictions are that it's important to tip well in restaurants, and **churlish** to drive through residential neighborhoods late at night with my music blasting loud enough to wake people up. I don't know if people think enough about the emotional significance of nature for any stance on it to be a commonly held conviction, and further, I'd posit that most people who *do* think about it often believe that nature *is* important. Further, is it really **"egregiously"** (outstandingly, shockingly) incorrect to think that people are not emotionally influenced by their surroundings? That seems a bit extreme. Because these claims aren't really central to the argument in the essay, they get no supporting evidence. They're just left hanging out there, waiting to be refuted. I doubt our writer really believes these things, so I wonder why he includes them.

Do you see what's happening here? The writer is trying to open the essay by making a grand, sweeping statement about life and universal truth, but all that's really happening is that he's giving his readers reasons to disagree with him *before he even gets to his thesis statement*. I'm arguing with the premises he's introducing as a contrast to his thesis! As a reader, even though I agree with the general thesis that people's emotional state can be influenced by their surroundings, I'm already thinking of reasons to disagree with this essay. Which means I'm on high alert for weak points in the argument. Which means I'm going to find some. This essay would be stronger if it just got to the thesis. This is where the 4 on organization and focus comes from.

Moving right along. The "evidence" in this essay is all **fabricated**. As you know, I'm against making up evidence, even though doing so is not against the rules and won't necessarily cost you points. I'm against it because it's too easy to dismiss an argument when its two pieces of evidence basically boil down to two simple characters with generally angry **dispositions** who are **placated** by nature. A reader who's looking for a reason to disagree can easily come up with two other fictional characters who get really angry when they're in the forest—maybe someone who witnessed his father's murder in a forest, and goes into a complete rage whenever he sees a tree.

The other reason making up evidence is a bad idea is that, as detailed as you try to make it, it's difficult to stay consistent with yourself. Note how, in the first example, Albert Wood is a horrible person who kills his dog and picks fights with strangers, but then learns to mellow out when he goes into the woods. However, only *after* he mellows out does he become an army general and a famous warrior. Seems **incongruous** to me.

I'm nitpicking here, admittedly, but I do so to make a point: the reason this essay scored relatively high is that this writer has a firm grasp on the written word, not that his evidence was fabricated. The argument isn't *bad*—I gave it a 5—but it's dragging a good writer's score down, not pulling it up.

Sample essay 3.2

Scientists and cognitive psychologists have confirmed through repeated experiments and studies that one's personality is both the result of genetic traits inherited from his or her biological parents and the social environment that he or she has been exposed and become accustomed to. One's personality is largely the result of the emotions and actions of one after he or she has been put in a situation. Because emotions make up a person's personality and their environment plays a crucial role in influencing his or her personality, it is acceptable to say that one's emotional wellbeing depends largely on one's environment.

One paradigm in which this case is abundantly clear is in the life and actions of a man named Ted Kascynzki, who is more famously known as the Unabomber. As a child, he was a prodigy. He had mastered advanced math by the time he was in high school and was accepted into Harvard at the tender age of 16. At this point his emotional wellbeing began to deteriorate. He was made fun of in high school and at Harvard for being younger than his classmates and odd. If he had been with children his own age much of the bullying may not have occurred. He was also involved in very high-pressure situations as a young child. As a prodigy, he had immense expectations thrust upon him and he was included in a study conducted by psychologists that were researching the effects of stress on young people's brains. This type of social environment contributed greatly to the deterioration of his social wellbeing. His environment had been one with copious amounts of stress and intolerance, which largely contributed to the dangerous and illegal activities of his adult years. The life of the Unabomber clearly shows that one's environment affects one's social wellbeing greatly.

Another paradigm in which this is abundantly clear is in the case of Ted Philips. This man was born to two drug addicts, but he surrounded himself with friends and adults that supported him and allowed him to excel in life. Philips' environment was one filled with love and friendship even though he had been born into a life of poverty and suffering. In contrast to Kascynzki, he had made friends in school and had thus been popular. Philips' cool demeanor and intelligence has allowed him to become one of the most successful men in America. He surrounded himself with good people and good came from him. He now helps lead a Fortune 500 company and participates in many philanthropic events.

In addition to genetics, one's environment influences one's emotional wellbeing the most. The stories, lives and works of Kascynzki and Phillips clearly demonstrate the relationship between one's environment and one's social health. In one case the environment benefited the man and in the other it helped deteriorate his social health, but in both cases their social wellbeing was affected immensely by their environment.

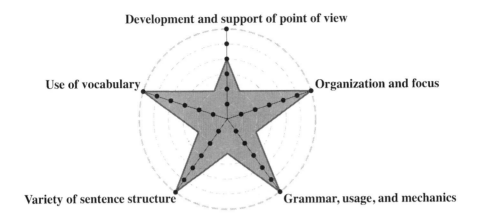

In giving this essay an 11, I'm saying that I think a grader *might* give you a 6, which means I think it'd have a shot at a 12. But I'm also saying I can see why a grader would give it a 5, so two harsh graders could also combine to give this a 10. The cookie crumbles that way, sometimes.

Here's why it's not a home run: the writer cites a convincing piece of evidence in the Unabomber (and makes a valiant effort at spelling Kaczynski) but the second piece of evidence is awfully vague. This is the problem with making things up—it's hard to be super specific. Anyone talking about a real life CEO would name the Fortune 500 firm he presides over. And how about some specifics about his parents? What was their drug of choice? What happened to them? While I'm at it, how about some more details about his philanthropic activities? Does he give to substance abuse counseling centers because of his own history? This isn't a drag on the score because Ted Philips is made up—it's a drag on the score because the writer doesn't really tell us much about Ted Philips.

In a situation like this, it's better to squeeze a strong piece of evidence for all it's worth. Our writer could have gone into much more detail about Ted Kaczynski, which would have made the essay much stronger. I'd like to see an argument that his physical environment and social isolation in his cabin contributed to his "dangerous and illegal" activities long after the stressful academic environment was behind him. Also, the essay never really says that the Unabomber *did*. Chances are good any adult reader remembers the events, but those details are relevant to the argument, and such specificity an important element in a high scoring essay. The writer of this essay gave good details in the beginning (naming Harvard, etc.) but then rushed off to talk about a fictional businessman instead of detailing a series of bombings that had the whole nation on edge. The truth, in this case, is so much more sensational than fiction!

Bottom line: this essay isn't bad, but it would have been stronger with a deep analysis of the Unabomber, rather than a shallower treatment of him, and a weakly fabricated example.

I generally like to see two pieces of evidence, but if you can write two strong pages about one, you shouldn't cut it short just to add another, weaker piece of evidence.

Sample essay 3.3

Imagine yourself in the deep forests, or the snowy mountains, or whatever pastoral paradise tickles your fancy. Or, if you like, looking at a masterpiece of sculpture, or listening to your very favorite song. You would take joy and contentment from these experiences, just as you would take an ill humor from a dissonant note in a symphony or a sleet storm in the summer. A person's environment, as it has the power to bring or dispel happiness, has a direct effect on his or her emotional wellbeing.

A recent experience of mine has led me to this conclusion. My high school is located in a national park, buffered by beaches to the east and west. Every day, riding the school bus, we pass sandy dunes and egrets sunning themselves by the bay. At lunchtime, my friends and I go outside and talk under the trees. You can smell the salt in the air and, in heavy winds, hear the waves crashing into the shore. I have always found this relaxing, and the proximity I feel to nature on any given day puts me into a good mood.

Unfortunately, that proximity to nature that my friends and I so love recently turned on us. Hurricane Sandy, when it struck this summer, destroyed much of the park and rendered all the buildings there inhabitable. Our school has relocated to a building in a busy town, right off of the Garden State Parkway. Confined indoors in a setting that nobody would describe as serene, I find myself more easily depressed. I have noticed this in others as well: clouds of doom descend easily, fogging even the most sunny personalities. Nobody focuses on academics or other activities quite as much as before, and even empty rooms seem somehow congested.

Repairs are underway, and we will return to the beaches next year. And of course, I keep in mind how lucky we are to have not been further damaged. However, this experience has brought me to a firm conclusion: people are happier when they're in a natural environment. Surrounded by concrete, everything slows down and people struggle to muster up motivation. For a true sense of wellbeing, you need a strong connection to the world around you and an environment that makes you smile.

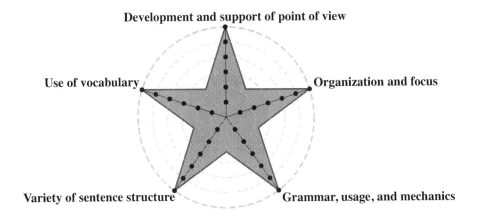

This essay is really nicely done. It states a clear thesis in the first paragraph ("A person's environment...has a direct effect on his or her emotional wellbeing") and then it doesn't stray from its purpose or waiver in support of its claim. And it doesn't rely on tired old material—the writer writes about what he knows! Further, he does stick to a classic 4-paragraph structure, but he gives himself and his style room to breathe, which is precisely what a strong writer should do—be conscious of structure, but seek opportunities within it to flex a bit.

As for the Essay Star, the writer displays mastery in all areas. I think it's obvious why in a bunch of the categories, but let me highlight the "Development and support of point of view" category. If you're particularly **dogmatic** about the essay skeleton, you might be concerned that there's only one piece of evidence. That's true, of course. But it's a deeply developed piece of evidence, and it does one of my favorite things: it addresses the writer's thesis from two angles! First, the writer describes how the original environment of his school made him happy. Then he explains about how the new environment makes him sad. In a way, his essay describes an experiment in which one variable, his school environment, was changed, and sure enough, that affected his mood. Could you argue with him, or suggest that maybe his mood was more affected by other factors (like Sandy) than he's letting on? Of course. But as far as SAT essays go, I'd say this feels like a very honest assessment of a lesson he's recently learned.

Since even the highest scoring essays can be improved, let me point out one stylistic decision the writer might want to rethink: *I'm not all that fond of addressing the reader directly.* Here, the writer tells the reader to imagine being in a **bucolic** setting, or looking at a nice sculpture, or whatever. The writer does a nice job of giving the reader some autonomy to picture a scene she finds pleasurable, but he's still asking the reader to fill in a blank. Rather than assuming a grader cares enough to actively participate in his essay, the writer might want to try something like this: "Some prefer deep forests; others prefer snowy mountaintops. Still others..." This minor revision would make the essay a bit less vulnerable to an unimaginative grader, but would still achieve the purpose of setting up the thesis.

Again, I really like this essay. It's a strong argument, and a nice example of a top-scoring essay that resembles the structure I advocate, but takes some **liberties** with it too.